CRITIQUES OF RESEARCH
IN THE SOCIAL SCIENCES

CRITIQUES OF RESEARCH IN THE SOCIAL SCIENCES

An Appraisal of Thomas and Znaniecki's
The Polish Peasant in Europe and America

BY

HERBERT BLUMER

WITH A NEW INTRODUCTION BY THE AUTHOR

With statements by William I. Thomas
and Florian Znaniecki, a panel discussion,
and summary and analysis by Read Bain

Transaction Books
New Brunswick, New Jersey

Library of Congress Catalog Number: 78-62685
ISBN: 0-87855-312-6 (cloth); 0-87855-694-X (paper)
Printed in the United States of America
Originally published in 1939 by the Social Science Research
Council.

Library of Congress Cataloging in Publication Data

Blumer, Herbert, 1900-
    An appraisal of Thomas and Znaniecki's The Polish peasant in
Europe and America.

    (Social science classics series)
    Reprint of the 1939 ed. published by Social Science Research
Council, New York, which was issued as no. 1 in Critiques of
research in the social sciences and as no. 44 in the Council's
Bulletin.
    Includes index.
    1. Thomas, William Isaac, 1863-1947. The Polish peasant in
Europe and America. 2. Znaniecki, Florian, 1882-1958, joint
author. The Polish peasant in Europe and America. 3.
Sociology—Methodology. I. Title. II. Series. III. Series: Critiques
of research in the social sciences ; 1. IV. Series: Social Science
Research Council. Bulletin ; 44.
HD728.T5623 1979   301.45'19'18504   78-62685
ISBN 0-87855-312-6
ISBN 0-87855-694-X pbk.

INTRODUCTION TO THE TRANSACTION EDITION

HERBERT BLUMER

The republication of my critique of *The Polish Peasant in Europe and America* provides an opportunity to comment on several crucial methodological issues which continue to plague sociology and social psychology. My critique, which was published in 1939, was prepared in response to a request of the Executive Committee of the Social Science Research Council. That committee had felt that the social sciences could benefit from a searching examination of the methodological character of outstanding pieces of research in several social sciences. In the case of sociology, the sociologists who were consulted agreed overwhelmingly that Thomas and Znaniecki's *Polish Peasant* was by far the most distinguished research study in their field. My critique of this work was regarded as sufficiently important to warrant a conference of eminent scholars to discuss the methodological issues that I had raised. The critique, the conference discussions, and a few separate commentaries are reproduced in the current publication.

Before addressing the methodological problems which, as I say, continue to haunt sociology, it is of some interest to reflect on the general way in which *The Polish Peasant* is viewed today, approximately forty years after my critique and some sixty years after the study. My impression is that sociologists who have come on the scene since World War

[v]

II have very little familiarity with the work and would be hard put to identify even a few of the many vital matters that it considered. This absence of even a modicum of firsthand familiarity with the work is all the more surprising in view of the exalted position which *The Polish Peasant* had in American sociology in the period from 1920 to 1940. There is no doubt that in the 1920s and 1930s, *The Polish Peasant* was viewed extensively in sociological circles at the finest exhibit of advanced sociological research and theoretical analysis. That the work should have moved so drastically and so quickly from this central position of sociological concern poses a most interesting problem for sociologists of knowledge. The shift cannot be attributed, as some might naively assume, to a displacement of a melioristic interest by a scientific interest; *The Polish Peasant* was actually a huge scholarly effort to find out what was going on in contemporary human society in place of being a plan for the reform of human society. Nor can the loss of sociological interest in *The Polish Peasant* be ascribed to a charge that the group life and the group problems with which it was concerned are no longer a part of our contemporary world. Such a charge has no foundation whatsoever, since the work was very clearly focused on the profound changes taking place in modern group life and human experience—the shift from rural, agricultural life to urban, industrial life and the mingling of peoples from diverse cultural backgrounds. Indeed, it should be pointed out that Thomas chose the Polish people for study not because of any special interest in them, but rather as a convenient group for the isolation of the processes of social change at work in modern society. Further, it cannot be said with any justification that sociologists of the present generation have lost interest in *The Polish Peasant* because

[vi]

the work does not present an integrated and carefully thought-out body of social theory; to the contrary, *The Polish Peasant* contains a theoretical scheme of the nature of human group life that is comprehensive, elaborate, logical, and very clear. Nor, finally, is the loss of sociological interest in *The Polish Peasant* to be explained by an alleged absence of empirical data that give support and meaning to the extensive social theory presented by the authors. The contrary is, of course, the case; probably no sociological study anywhere reflects greater diligence and exhaustiveness in gathering relevant empirical data than was done in the case of *The Polish Peasant*.

We have then in *The Polish Peasant* an extensive piece of sociological research, probably more extensive than any other ever done; one devoted to the study and analysis of the central theoretical problems of change taking place in modern society; one operating with a comprehensive and carefully thought-out theoretical framework; one gathering and using a body of empirical data that in size and careful selection towers over what is usually presented in sociological research; and one that enjoyed unrivaled acclaim of sociologists of its period. Why should such a work largely disappear from sociological concern? A major portion of the answer probably lies in the puzzling and undeciphered shifts of interest that take place generally in human group life—a shifting process that most sociologists are scarcely aware of, and that very few, if any, ever study. Much has happened in the half century that has passed since the heyday of *The Polish Peasant*: new figures, new points of view, new claims, new pretensions, new controversies, new theories, new tastes, and new preoccupations. In the vast selective process which is underway in this churning arena, the redirection of attention and interest is common. I believe that *The Polish Peasant* has been caught in this process and has not fared well in it. But beyond this loss in importance caused by the shifting of interests, *The Polish Peasant* has ceased to be a model of research procedure and theoretical analysis because of its methodological stance. Since this methodological stance lay at the heart of my critique of *The Polish Peasant* and constituted the central concern of the subsequent conference of scholars, I would like to identify it and show the inescapable issues to which it gave rise.

The basic premise of Thomas and Znaniecki's approach in *The Polish Peasant* was that human group life consists of the interplay of "objective" and "subjective" factors. Both of these factors are declared to be present in any and every instance of individual and collective social action, and thus both factors must be included in explanations of group life. Let me explain this premise as simply as possible. It means that in any and every instance of social action (such as a person buying food, attending church, entering into marriage, robbing a victim, studying for an examination, or a political group organizing a campaign, or a legislature enacting a law) the acting individual or group has to deal with a set of outside circumstances, particularly a set of group rules as to how to act; these circumstances and social rules constitute the objective setting of the given line of action. At the same time, the actor (whether it be an individual, an organized collectivity, or an aggregate of individuals) approaches these objective conditions with a set of subjective dispositions, such as wishes, appetites, hopes, fears, aversions, intentions, and plans. Social action, or what people do, results from the combination of the objective conditions and the subjective dispositions; that is to say that a person acts toward something that has a group meaning (the objective factor), yet he acts toward that thing in response to how he feels about it and how he sizes it up (the subjective factor). Thomas and Znaniecki lumped all of the subjective factors under the central concept of "attitudes" and the objective conditions under the central concept of "values." The study and analysis of group life and of the action of actors has to be made in terms of the joint play of attitudes and values. The implication of this premise for the study of social change (with which Thomas and Znaniecki were predominantly concerned) should become readily apparent. As long as the values and the attitudes incident to any line of action are *fixed* in relation to each other, the line of action remains constant and stable. Contrariwise, change in action is bound to occur if the actor who possesses a set of fixed attitudes encounters new values or social rules, or if the actor brings new attitudes to bear upon fixed values; in other words, social change is to be traced to either a change in values (objective factors) or a change in attitudes (subjective dispositions), recognizing that both of these factors are necessarily jointly present in every instance of social action. Thomas and Znaniecki riveted this thought in their idea of "laws of social becoming"; a law of social becoming consisted of a given new attitude playing upon a given established value, or a new value playing on an established attitude.

Thomas and Znaniecki used this basic premise of an interplay of attitudes and values to develop their *procedure* for the study of human group life. Since social action results from the way in which the actor sees and interprets the objective conditions with which he has to deal, it is necessary to employ a method that catches his perception and his interpretation. The research instrument that

[ix]

would do this, that would allow the identification of the subjective element, was for Thomas and Znaniecki the "human document." Thus, the use of the human document became the predominant research procedure employed by the authors in identifying and analyzing the profound social changes taking place in the peasant society in Poland and the profound changes in human conduct and social institutions taking place among Polish immigrants in American cities. The primary human documents that they used consisted of (1) vast numbers of letters written back and forth, chiefly inside of family circles, (2) a large number of varied life histories and autobiographical accounts, and (3) a large number of communications from Polish people to newspapers in Poland and in the United States. Students who turn to *The Polish Peasant*, as I hope many of the newer generation will be led to do, will find an abundance, almost a superabundance, of such documentary materials used by the authors to carry out their analysis.

Now, to return to the line of thought which I was expressing a few paragraphs back, I suspect that the major explanation of why *The Polish Peasant* has vanished from its previous position of outstanding importance is due precisely to its premise that (1) one has to include the subjective element in the sociological analysis of human society, and (2) that one catches this element through human documents such as letters and life histories. American sociology since World War II has shifted very markedly from both of these positions. It is believed today that generalizations are to be sought and that analyses are to be made in the form of relations and correlations between "objective" variables. Further, even when sociological scholars are sensitive to so-called subjective factors, they

[x]

are highly unlikely to rely on letters and life histories to catch such factors. In short, the main stream of contemporary sociological thought is not merely indifferent to Thomas and Znaniecki's basic premise but seems to be vigorously opposed to the premise. To illustrate, I find it very difficult to conceive that any contemporary dispenser of research funds, whether it be a private foundation or a governmental agency, would give any serious consideration to a research proposal that was drawn up in terms of Thomas and Znaniecki's basic premise. Indeed, it is not difficult to imagine the guffaws that would greet a contemporary submission of an application for funds such as Thomas and Znaniecki had in mind in their study of the Polish peasant. The reviewers would ask the following questions. What is your problem? What is your population? What is your representative sample of that population? How are you going to develop that sample? What is your control group? What are your variables? What is your hypothesis? What are the instruments that you are going to use to get your data? Do your instruments provide quantitative data? Thomas would have been too urbane and courageous a person to quail before a barrage of such contemporary questions; he would probably have just turned away in a spirit of righteous disgust. At any rate, it is safe to say that if he had had to rely on the standards of contemporary fund granting agencies, his monumental study ("monumental" has been the customary characterization of *The Polish Peasant*) would never have been made.

This startling surmise should force us to an *examination* and a *reexamination* of what I refer to as the basic methodological issues set by *The Polish Peasant*. These issues continue to lie at the core of sociological inquiry despite the current propensity to ignore them or to detour around them. An examination of the issues was undertaken in my

[xi]

critique and in the conference on my critique. A reexamination is in order, in the light of close to forty years of development since the critique and the conference. Let me first summarize the issues that were brought out by my critique and in the conference discussion of the critique.

In my rather extensive critique I sought to make the following points. *First*, Thomas and Znaniecki had sustained rather decisively their contention that social action springs from so-called subjective dispositions and that, consequently, such dispositions have to be included in any sociological analysis of social action. *Second*, their claim of establishing laws of social change ("laws of social becoming") had no substance because of basic deficiencies in their concepts of "attitude" and "value." *Third*, the human documents that they used (letters, life histories, etc.) did not either prove or disprove the validity of their generalizations and theoretical declarations. Yet, *fourth*, despite the failure of the human documents to meet the test of scientific criteria (representativeness of data, adequacy of data, reliability of data, and decisiveness of data) the documentary data did clarify and give support to theoretical assertions and, reciprocally, the theoretical assertions illuminated and clarified the data; this set an anomalous relation between theory and data in the use of human documents. It is interesting to note that the participants in the conference agreed that I had established the four points that I have specified in this paragraph. Consequently, as will be perceived by reading the verbatim account of the conference, the discussion turned largely to the dilemma which I posed in summing up my critique; namely, that on one hand, it is absolutely necessary to include the relevant subjective elements in a sociological analysis of human society, yet, on the other hand, the instruments (human documents) for getting such subjective

[xii]

elements do not allow us to meet the customary criteria for scientific data.

The reader can follow the discussion as it took place in the conference with regard to the dilemma which I posed. The conferees were very able scholars from social and psychological science; they had rich backgrounds of diversified experience; they were sophisticated and learned in their respective theoretical perspectives; most of them had extensive experience in sociological and psychological research. It is most interesting to see how, with this enviable equipment, they addressed the central methodological dilemma. I put the matter in this way to emphasize that the methodological issues that were raised in the consideration of *The Polish Peasant* are still with us—with us in a way that is perhaps more telling today than it was a half century ago. It is in order to reconsider these methodological questions.

Our reconsideration will deal with three fundamental methodological questions: (1) is it true that genuine sociological analysis of human group life has to include subjective factors; (2) if so, are "human documents" a necessary or appropriate instrument for catching subjective factors; and (3) if human documents are a required research instrument do they meet the criteria of a "scientific" instrument. The reader should keep in mind that *The Polish Peasant* was grounded methodologically on an affirmative answer to all three of these questions. I wish to consider each of the three questions.

1. The Place of Subjective Factors in Sociological Analysis.

Thomas and Znaniecki are unequivocal in their contention that subjective factors are an integral part of human group life and that, accordingly, they must be included in

[xiii]

sociological analyses and propositions. Their thesis, as stated above, is that actors bring subjective dispositions (impulses, wishes, hopes, fears, anxieties, intentions, and plans) to the objective social settings in which they act; activity results from the combination of the given subjective dispositions and the given objective conditions. This central position of subjective dispositions is to be noted, especially, in Thomas and Znaniecki's theory of social change. According to part of this theory, any *new* objective social arrangement comes into being only as a result of the play of new subjective dispositions on the previous social arrangement. As I have said above, the participants in the conference dealing with my critique of *The Polish Peasant* did not take exception to Thomas and Znaniecki's contention as to the unavoidable place and role of subjective dispositions in human group life. Yet, today, this contention is widely rejected or ignored by sociologists. It becomes advisable, accordingly, to reexamine the issue posed by Thomas and Znaniecki's contention, namely, the question of whether subjective dispositions have to be a part, *pari passu*, of sociological analysis.

There are two points of view held by many sociologists today which lead automatically to the exclusion of subjective factors from sociological study and explanation. One of these is the "behavioristic" position that scientific inquiry requires the use of only "objective" data; in accordance with this view, all subjective ("mentalistic") items such as wishes, purposes, hopes, etc. must be rigorously excluded from research procedure and from theoretical propositions. The other widespread point of view is that a human society is an entity in its own right, consisting of structural parts that transcend individuals, and operating in the form of interaction between these societal parts.

[xiv]

This is essentially the premise of so-called macrosociology. In studying human society from this point of view, the sociologist must remain on the societal level, confining himself to objective relations between societal factors and avoiding any kind of reductionism, such as introducing individual psychological factors into his scheme.

Both of these widely held positions are at odds with Thomas and Znaniecki's theoretical point of view as presented in *The Polish Peasant*. The point of view of Thomas and Znaniecki, even though not carefully thought through by them, is that a human society consists of people engaging in activities and having experiences which prepare them to engage in activity. The essence of a society is constituted by what people in that society *do*. The theoretical analysis of social action, or of what people do, is the key to the analysis of human society. Now, as mentioned above, Thomas and Znaniecki saw human social action as consisting of how people who are guided or impelled by subjective dispositions meet and handle the social situations in which they are placed. This position of Thomas and Znaniecki sets very clearly the issue that has to be considered. The issue can be put in the form of two questions: (1) is it true that human society exists basically in the form of social action, and (2) is it true that human social action is in the form of people with subjective dispositions meeting social situations. Let us consider each question.

There can be little question that, currently, the predominant majority of sociologists locate the essence of human society not in social action but, instead, in preceding conditions which are regarding as producing social action. The two conditions customarily taken as producing, hence as explaining, social action are "social structure" and "culture." The general view is that a human society exists in

the form of a structure and a culture, and that the behavior of people in such a society is to be seen as an expression of the structure and culture. Structure and culture are
put in the primary position; social action is placed in a
secondary position and treated as a product derived from
structure and culture. This widespread point of view in
current sociology is the reverse of the position implied by
Thomas and Znaniecki's methodological premise; for
them, social action is primary and thus must be the starting
point of analysis. The difference between these two points
of view lay at the very core of the methodological dilemma
of present sociology. In my judgment, the position of
Thomas and Znaniecki, even though worked out rather
poorly by them, is much more defensible than is the contrary view that is so widely held among sociologists today.
There are a number of basic reasons why I think that this
is true. Let me spell them out briefly.

First, "social structures" and "cultural patterns" are
abstractions *derived from* the observation of what people in
a given society do. Action comes first and is used as the
basis for constructing given schemes of social structure
and normative codes. One way in which I think that this
can be appreciated is to imagine a society in which there is
no action, in which, so to speak, the positions of people are
frozen; under such a condition, there would be no possibility of ascertaining the relation between people or of identifying any social rules that presumably govern such relations. Structural relations and normative codes are derived
from the observation and analysis of ongoing activities. It
is true, of course, that one may turn around and ascribe
this or that given instance of social action to a given structural relationship or to a given set of norms, but this does
not challenge the thesis of the primacy of action. A human

[xvi]

society must be seen in the first instance as consisting of living, acting people; group life consists of their ongoing activities. Social action, in place of a derived structure and normative code, should be the starting point for the analysis of human society. To reverse this arrangement, to start from social structure and culture, is to commit what Whitehead has called the "Fallacy of the Misplaced Concrete."

A *second* and closely allied reason for starting analysis with social action is that the acting units in human societies are *always* human beings—either (1) an individual human being, (2) an aggregate of individual human beings, or (3) an organization or collective of human beings. In their analysis of human society, sociologists are accustomed to designate societal units—such as institutions, communities, associations, organizations, families, gangs, and population aggregates—as the entities that are engaged in action. There is the danger that in working with such supraindividual units, sociologists may lose sight of the fact that such units always turn out to be human beings in one or the other of their individual, aggregate, or organized collective forms. This frightfully simple observation should force the direction of scholarly attention to the action of human actors, either individually or collectively, when one analyzes human society.

Accepting the premise that human society exists basically and in the first instance in the form of social action, we should now consider the question of what kind of picture we get when we analyze human social action. The premise of Thomas and Znaniecki (which, to repeat, they did not develop very well) is that human actors *always* act *in social situations*, that is to say, that the scene of action is always constituted by an exterior setting or arrangement

[xvii]

and that the actors are always oriented and guided in such situations by subjective dispositions. I can find no fault with the premise. I would ask any critic who is disposed to reject the premise to give a *single* empirical instance of (1) a human social act taking place outside of a social situation and/or (2) the given actor not having a disposition that underlies his social act. I find it impossible to identify, or conceive of, such an instance. (It should be noted here that social action is distinctly different from physiological reflexes.)

In the absence of any grounds for believing the Thomas and Znaniecki premise to be faulty, it follows that the sociological analysis of human society would have to include subjective dispositions. The logic here is impeccable: (1) group life consists *always* of the action of human actors; (2) such action *always* takes place as an adjustment of human actors to social situations; and (3) action in situations is *always* in the form of actors expressing their dispositions. Ergo, sociological research has to ferret out the play of subjective dispositions, and sociological propositions have to incorporate the record of that play.

What is current sociological thought going to do with this seeming irrefutable logical scheme? To cast it aside on the ground that it is "subjective" or "mentalistic," as the behaviorist would do, is an arbitrary doctrinaire act. To ignore the scheme, (as the macro-sociologist does) on the ground that the supra-units of a human society operate on a societal level that transcends subjective factors, is to beg the very question which is at issue. Sociology has to face up to the issue that is posed by the Thomas and Znaniecki premise. If it is true that social action is the basic stuff of a human society and that social action inescapably incorporates subjective dispositions of the actors, sociological

[xviii]

study would require a methodological approach that respects these features. To respect these features would require the sociological scholar to always give attention to the play of the subjective factors that are involved in the area of social action which he is studying, and also to incorporate that play in his explanations and propositions.

I have to pursue this matter a bit further since there is another widespread view to the effect that, while subjective factors are present in what sociologists study, these factors can be ignored on "heuristic" grounds. This argument may take several different forms, such as that subjective factors are of negligible importance, or that they are actually determined and controlled by an initiating objective factor, or that they cancel out each other in an aggregate of acting individuals. In either case, it is believed that one can ignore them and confine oneself solely to relations between objective factors. In support of such a "heuristic" position, the advocates may point to one or another proposition of human action which, while not denying the presence of subjective dispositions, makes unnecessary the specification of such dispositions. A convenient illustration is the well-known Gresham's law in economics. This law states that the introduction of poor money drives good money out of circulation. It would be acknowledged that this occurs because people *prefer* good money and hence hoard such money. Yet, it is argued that this preference for good money operates in such an automatic and fixed way that it is not necessary to incorporate it as a term in the law; one can just say that one objective factor (the introduction of poor money) leads inevitably to the other objective factor (the disappearance of good money). This kind of heuristic argument, in my judgment, provides a frail basis for concluding that one can ignore subjective factors

[xix]

in the sociological study of relations between objective factors. Instead, the proper position is to make sure that subjective dispositions are inconsequential, or are actually predetermined by a designated objective factor, or cancel out each other in an aggregate of individuals. These possibilities need to be verified by actual empirical validation and not assumed to be true in an *a priori* fashion. Had such a caution been exercised by sociologists, we would be spared the many erroneous declarations on the supposed objective consequences of such objective factors (to cite a few of many) as industrialization, urbanization, demographic change, centralization of management, and an increase of the size of the police force. There is need of respecting Thomas and Znaniecki's thesis that such objective factors are *always* met by subjective dispositions of the people on whom the objective factors are playing, and that significant differences in behavior result from differences in such subjective dispositions.

Before leaving this discussion of the need of including subjective factors in sociological analyses, it is advisable to explain briefly a basic weakness to be noted in Thomas and Znaniecki's position, a weakness that has very important methodological consequences. I did not identify this weakness in my critique of *The Polish Peasant* and hence, regretfully, it was never discussed in the conference. The weakness stems from the two different ways in which Thomas and Znaniecki spoke of the subjective factor, without being aware of the difference between the two. On one hand and to a major degree, they regard the subjective factor to exist in the form of a disposition which is already shaped and established, such as a wish, a hope, an aversion, or an intention. The actor meets his situations with such subjective dispositions, which are already formed; his

[handwritten marginal notes:] But "live" subjective dispositions may not sufficiently account for how they originated — so how to account for them?

action results from the combination of such dispositions and the objective factors in the situations. This view of the subjective factor is very definitely evident in Thomas and Znaniecki's fundamental concept of "attitudes"; the attitude is already there with a fashioned shape as it enters into relations with "values" (the objective factor). An example would be the proposition that tyrannical behavior by a Polish father (a value) playing on a son's feeling of family solidarity (an attitude) produces submissive behavior on the part of the son. One can see under this view of the subjective that subjective dispositions are given the status of completed or formed entities. The task of scholarly inquiry is to ferret out the dispositions and relate them to the relevant objective factors.

The other picture of the subjective factor that emerges from Thomas and Znaniecki's discussion is quite different. It is that the subjective factor is not an already established attitude that is brought into play but, instead, an ongoing contingent process—a process in which the actor is engaged in interpreting a situation so as to be able to act in it. This is what the authors speak of as "defining a situation"—a pregnant conception which, regrettably, they never thought through. The possession of a disposition with which one approaches a situation is a very different matter than the subsequent process of sizing up the situation and deciding what to do in it. These two matters should not be confused and lumped together as Thomas and Znaniecki unwittingly do in their treatment. Each calls for a different set of data and a different type of analysis. In defining a situation, and actor is not merely releasing an already formed disposition; instead, he is taking account of different facets of his situation (including, usually, his own disposition), judging their relevance, and projecting

[xxi]

forward in his imagination a sketch of a possible line of action before he engages in it. One cannot cover this process by referring to an antecedent disposition, such as is done in theories of motivation. Defining the situation stands apart as a subjective process in its own right. I am not concerned here with undertaking the sorely needed analysis of what is involved in "defining a situation." (I am engaged in writing a book that is to deal with this process.) My interest is *first* to point out that Thomas and Znaniecki failed to see it as a distinct subjective factor that was different from their concept of an "attitude," and *second* to note that it requires a mode of study quite different from the study of a disposition. *The Polish Peasant* leaves us, so to speak, with the need of recognizing that there are two kinds of subjective factors that are indigenous in human social action. The methodological problem of how to get at each of them cannot be dodged by sociologists, if sociologists wish to respect their empirical world. I wish now to turn to the second general question which I raised earlier, namely, the suitability of "human documents" for catching and identifying subjective factors.

2. *Are Human Documents an Appropriate Research Instrument for Locating Subjective Factors?*

In *The Polish Peasant*, Thomas and Znaniecki speak of human documents as the preeminent instrument for the study of human society, particularly of social change. Today, this contention would appear ludicrous to many sociologists—I suspect to the great majority of them. Very few contemporary sociologists who are concerned with studying and analyzing the vast process of social change would seek their data, as did Thomas and Znaniecki, in individual life histories, or in series of letters between kinfolk and others, or in letters written to newspapers. The sociologist who wishes to get "subjective" data relies on a very different array of sources. He would most likely use survey research as his chief instrument; or he might use some other questionnaire procedure; or he might employ some form of interviewing; or he might engage in clinical studies; or he might use attitude or personality tests; or he might set up a simulated study; or he might undertake a controlled laboratory experiment; or he might seek to engage in so-called participant observation. These are the kinds of procedures which rank high today in getting at the supposed experience of actors. The marked difference between them and human documents as used by Thomas and Znaniecki poses the problem of the suitability of human documents for locating subjective factors. This is the problem that I wish to consider.

Our discussion should begin with the simple but necessary observation that any research procedure which can tell us something about the subjective orientation of human actors has a claim to scholarly consideration. Thus, all of the techniques mentioned in the previous paragraph qualify for use in some respect. Indeed, there are literally scores of additional procedures that seek in one or another way to get at subjective factors. In the light of all of these claimants for use, what is to be said on behalf of the employment of human documents as advocated by Thomas and Znaniecki? Why should such human documents be used as a primary way of identifying the play of subjective factors, particularly in the light of the disdainful way in which they are viewed by contemporary sociologists and social psychologists? I wish to explain what seem to be the

[xxiii]

merit and justification of human documents as used in *The Polish Peasant*.

As mentioned previously, the principal human documents used in *The Polish Peasant* were letters and life histories. Their merit comes in large part from the fact that they are forms of "naturalistic" study. By naturalistic study, I refer to the observation of a given area of happening in terms of its natural or actual character, as opposed to the observation of a surrogate or substitute form of that area of happening. Many, indeed most, modes of study of human group life do not study that life as it is going on naturally. Instead, they deal with some kind of contrived, imported, or constructed representation of that area of happening. This can be seen very clearly in the case of a laboratory experiment which is arranged to reproduce some form of behavior from real life but is not that real life. The difference is also evident in the study of simulated behavior as against real behavior. The difference is also to be noted in the case of studies which focus on the *products* of what happens in place of observing the course of happenings that gave rise to the products; the predominant majority of sociological studies fall into this category. Also, conventional studies which start with a constructed model of what is to be studied and which make contact with the actual world through deductions from the model differ from naturalistic study. Also, a difference is to be noted in the case of studies which seek to reconstruct a picture of what happened and then proceed to study that reconstruction. Also, a clear difference exists between naturalistic study, and studies, such as survey research, which aim to provide an idea of how people *might* act as opposed to how they have acted or are acting. The same difference is likewise evident in studies which seek to measure attitudes or personality traits; they are not directed to the observation of what is actually in process in group life. A little reflection should make clear that, to an overwhelming extent, current sociological studies are not "naturalistic" in the sense of focusing inquiry and observation on the actual flow of human group life.

I am not interested here in comparing the respective merits of naturalistic studies of human life with "non-naturalistic" studies. I merely wish to assert that naturalistic study is fully justified, that it is very important, and that it requires modes of inquiry that will yield data on what is actually going on in the area of life under study. Now it is evident that Thomas and Znaniecki were very much concerned with a *naturalistic* study of what was actually taking place in the life of Polish peasants who were caught up in the social transformation under way in Poland and in American cities. The data which they sought referred to the actual process of change in experience which was taking place. Seen in this light, the letters and life histories on which they relied make a great deal of sense as sources of relevant data. By and large, the letters expressed the crucial experiences of their writers—the problems which confronted them, their concerns and their worries, their griefs and their triumphs, their apprehensions and their hopes, their unusual experiences and their efforts to meet them. We should bear in mind two additional considerations which add to the research merit of the letters. One is that the letters were dealing essentially with immediate experiences in the present and not with a far-removed reconstruction of such experiences, as happens for instance in writing memoirs; naturalistic research needs observations in, and of, the here and now. The other relevant consideration is that the letters were addressed by their writers to an audience which was very vital to them—their kinfolk in one instance and the *voice* of the community (newspapers) in the other instance. The role of the "audience" in shaping the presentation of personal experience is of great significance. In the case of the letters used in *The Polish Peasant*, the vital audience of the writers led to an expression of experience that lay at the core of the struggles of the Polish peasant and the Polish immigrant to meet and handle a new world. In the hands of a sensitive scholar, the letters depicted the new situations as seen by the writers; the feelings and intentions of the writers in the face of such new situations; the way in which the writers defined or interpreted these situations; and the ways in which they worked out their lines of action in the situations. A research instrument which yields such data to a scholar who is endeavoring to tease out the subjective factors in play in a changing social world should command recognition and respect. The use of letters by Thomas and Znaniecki should be seen in this light.

Life histories are also a means of the naturalistic observation of human experience in the context of group situations. Life histories may vary enormously in their value, many of them being essentially useless. But a well prepared life history in the hands of an informed and sensitive scholar can reveal significant data on the flow of situations in group life and on the way in which such situations are met. In addition, life histories permit one to identify the lines of formation which lead over time to the emergence of given personality types among individuals and given cultural patterns and social arrangements in group life. Thomas and Znaniecki's use of life histories exemplifies abundantly the possibilities of life histories as an instrument of naturalistic study. Anyone who has taken the time to read *The Polish Peasant* must remain impressed by the way in which life histories provide telling data for the analysis of group and individual transformation.

I trust that my few remarks are sufficient to make clear that letters and life histories proved to be incisive instruments for Thomas and Znaniecki. I am more interested here in pointing out that the discussion sets a broader and more important methodological problem. The problem has two parts: (1) how to delineate the character of naturalistic research as distinguished from nonnaturalistic research and (2) how to get at the area of subjective experience in the case of naturalistic studies of human group life.

Concerning the first of these two parts of the problem, I merely wish to say that there is nothing in print that represents a serious effort to distinguish between naturalistic and nonnaturalistic research into human group life. The matter has been ignored. Yet two kinds of research call for different modes of attack, different techniques of observation, different forms of recording data, and different kinds of analyses. I am sure that these differences are of great importance. The jumbling together of naturalistic and nonnaturalistic methods of study has resulted, in my judgment, in a large amount of methodological confusion, a confusion that is more harmful because it is unrecognized. We have, I think, a very inviting opportunity to make a methodological contribution of great significance by distinguishing in a clear-cut way between naturalistic and nonnaturalistic research and to draw out the implications of the difference.

The other part of the problem poses the question of how scholars are to get at the area of subjective experience in naturalistic studies of human group life. It is necessary in such studies to get data on how the actors approach their situations, see their situations, define their situations, and lay out lines of action in their situations. Obviously, the most suitable data on such matters have to be supplied by the actors, themselves, in the form of accounts of their experience. These naturalistic accounts constitute what Thomas and Znaniecki have in mind when they talk about "human documents." Clearly, the naturalistic accounts given by actors of their experiences could take many other forms than letters and life histories. The accounts could consist, for example, of recordings of conversations between those involved in a line of action (as in the case of a boy's gang or of a board of directors of a corporation); remarks of an actor as remembered by others; diaries; confessions; responses to interrogating; accounts from actors immediately after engaging in given actions; disclosures made under hypnosis; accounts of telephone conversations; and so forth. By construing human documents to cover all such kinds of records of the experience of actors in naturalistic situations, it is apparent that we are presented with the possibility of developing a kit of tools that go way beyond the human documents that were used and discussed by Thomas and Znaniecki. We very much need a careful exploration of this whole problem of human documents in the case of naturalistic studies of group life.

3. Do Human Documents Meet the Criteria of a Scientific Instrument?

Let us accept the premise that human documents in some form are indispensable for securing data in the naturalistic study of human group life. A legitimate question remains as to whether such documents meet the criteria expected of a scientific instrument. The questions to be faced are: (1) do human documents provide *representative* data, (2) are the data *adequate*, (3) are the data *reliable*, and (4) do the data allow *decisive validation* of proposed theoretical interpretations. In my critique of *The Polish Peasant*, I showed that the human documentary data submitted by Thomas and Znaniecki did not meet the test of each of these four criteria. The letters and the life histories were not drawn from an established representative sample; there was no way of telling whether the letters included all of the important subjective experiences of their writers bearing on their given actions; we do not know if the separate accounts given in the documents were honest and truthful; and it is evident that, in many instances, the documentary accounts allowed equally well for diverse and sometimes contradictory interpretations. These negative findings would seem on their face to explode any claim that human documents should be used in the sociological study of human group life. Indeed, the negative findings should have demolished the creditability and scientific standing of *The Polish Peasant*. However, I pointed out (and I believe established) that even though the human documents used in *The Polish Peasant* could not meet these four conventional criteria of a scientific mode of inquiry, the documents yielded data of unquestionably great value for the analysis of the life of the Polish peasants. More precisely, I pointed out that (1) the documentary data gave great intelligibility and support to Thomas and Znaniecki's theoretical propositions and that (2) in turn, the theoretical propositions gave a great deal of new and telling meaning to the data. In short, it was evident that there was an extensive and fruitful interaction between empirical data and theoretical propositions, an interaction that yielded an analysis of Polish peasant life that was truly monumental in both merit and extent.

Representativeness

The ordinary way to meet the criterion of the representative character of data is to secure a "representative" sample of the population under study. In Thomas and Znaniecki's study, this would be the Polish peasants. Yet this conventional approach turns out to be rather meaningless in the case of human documents. There are two major reasons for this. First, where documents already exist (as in the form of the letters used by Thomas and Znaniecki), it is apparent that the authors of the letters do not form, in any conventional sense, a representative sample of the population from which the authors came. What is to be done with the unknown portions of the population who write no letters or whose letters never came to light? Second, and more importantly, to try to meet the problem by choosing a representative sample of the population, and then getting the members in it to prepare the given kind of human documents that are sought would be essentially a worthless enterprise. It would be worthless because many persons are incapable of supplying the data that are being sought. Many, for example, could never write an informative letter, or a meaningful life history, or a revealing diary, or give a confession, or respond fruitfully to a probing interview. To depend on such people for relevant accounts of experience would amount to a nullification of one's study.

Now, what is to be done with this anomalous situation wherein the documents yielding essential data do not measure up to the standards of scientific instruments, yet where the data that are yielded are of unquestionably great value for an effective analysis of the vast process of social change that was under study. This was the dilemma with which I concluded my critique of *The Polish Peasant*. In turn, the dilemma and its implications became the central problem of the discussion at the conference. It is clear to me that the conference never succeeded in resolving the dilemma. And it is equally clear to me today, close to forty years later, that the dilemma has not been resolved at all during the intervening time. Sociologists have merely turned away from the dilemma. I think that in time sociologists will have to deal with the important methodological questions that are posed by the dilemma. I would like to identify these methodological questions and say a few words about them.

Let me begin by saying that the dilemma cannot be resolved by trying to force human documents (and hence their data) into a form that meets the four scientific criteria of representativeness, adequacy, reliability, and testability of propositions, as conventionally conceived. I am convinced that to hold documentary data rigidly to these criteria as conventionally conceived would be equivalent to robbing the data of their value. Since this comes to the heart of the methodological questions that I wish to pose, let me explain what I have in mind. I will consider each of the four criteria.

Let me pursue this thought by emphasizing that not all people who are involved in the given area of social action under study are equally involved, nor are they equally knowledgeable about what is taking place; hence they cannot be regarded as equally capable of supplying information on the form of social action under study. Some of the people, although involved in what is happening, are at the periphery of the happening; other people, even though in the main stream of what is happening, may be exceedingly poor observers of what is taking place around them. In either of these two cases, the people are poorly qualified to supply the data required by the study. To include them in a "representative sample" is to dilute or weaken the data that are needed in the study. Let me illustrate. Suppose that one is making a study of how labor unions in a given industrial sector come to engage in authorized labor strikes, and that one wishes to focus the study on the formation of this action from the standpoint of the actors who bring the strike into being. How would one get one's data? To go to the rank and file of the union would be to seek one's data from people who are uninformed about what really happened. Even staff members who are highly placed in the union bureaucracy may have only partial knowledge of what happened in reaching a decision on whether or not to strike. Further, some persons who may have been in the circle whose deliberations led to decisions to strike may have been poor observers of what was happening in the circle. All of these trite observations should help one to understand why a conventional "representative sample" of a population is no answer at all to the central question of how to make human documents representative.

If one is studying the formation of social action, the data that one needs have to refer to how the actors approach, see, define, and handle the situations in which they have to act. The "representativeness" of the data yielded by human documents has to be determined by considering the question of whether the data cover what is involved in the formation of the given action; representativeness must be sought, not in getting a representative sample of a given demographic population, but instead, in making sure that the authors of the human documents were knowledgeable about the formation of the given action under study. A half-dozen individuals with such knowledge constitute a far better "representative sample" than a thousand individuals who may be involved in the action that is being formed but who are not knowledgeable about that formation. I put the matter in this startling way to call attention to the fact that the use of human documents sets a markedly new and unsolved methodological problem of "representativeness"—a problem which sociologists across the board do not recognize, much less address.

Adequacy

Human documents that are used to identify the subjective factors and the subjective process in play in the formation of social action must meet the criterion of supplying adequate information on such factors and process. Yet to meet this requirement, the use of human documents must take a different form than in the case of conventional research instruments. The task in the ordinary research instrument is to identify as precisely as possible the "variables" which one is using and then make sure that one has adequate coverage of each variable. In the case of human documents, there is an additional need, namely, to search for and spot new and previously unrecognized factors that may be in play. This additional need calls for several things: the repeated reexamination of the given documents that are being used; the supplementation of such documents by other documents of the same sort (e.g., adding new letters to those already possessed); and the widening of one's inquiry to bring in other kinds of human documents (e.g., interrogations, group conversations, recollections by other participants). These simple points may seem boringly obvious. Yet they indicate that the problem of adequacy of data in the case of human documents is not to be met by the conventional routes of getting an adequate measurement of the variables that are used. Instead, a broad, flexible, and redirecting inquiry is needed. The methodology of such *exploratory* research has not been worked out at all; it poses an important challenge to our discipline.

Reliability

Scientific data are expected to be accurate and truthful, in the sense of being genuinely what they purport to be. Do the data yielded by human documents meet this expectation? Many critics charge that the authors of personal accounts can easily give free play to their imaginations, choose what they want to say, hold back what they do not want to say, slant what they wish, say only what they happen to recall at the moment, in short, to engage in both deliberate and unwitting deception. They argue, accordingly, that accounts yielded by human documents are not trustworthy. This charge must not be treated lightly. One can usually make a formidable case against almost every single documentary account, with the logical implication that the entire array of such accounts becomes suspect. I made this observation in my critique of *The Polish Peasant* in the case of the letters used by Thomas and Znaniecki. Yet, immediately, I was forced to recognize that when taken as a collective array, the letters supported one another in an unbelievably impressive way. What is one to do with such a finding? Is the trustworthiness of the data to be sought in the reliability of the separate account or in some sort of a transcending affirmation that comes from an aggregate of such accounts, each of which is open to doubt? I have never seen this important question addressed in the methodological discussions in our discipline.

A related kind of observation is in order, one based on an actual case with which I am familiar. A few decades ago a very able Chinese graduate student wrote a thesis on rural family life in the part of China from which he came. He included detailed life histories on about a dozen families in the area. It was later learned that he had manufactured these life histories. Yet, we were subsequently assured by three eminent Chinese scholars of family life in that area of China that the case histories were excellent realistic accounts that "rang true." The question may be asked, if the scholarly value of human accounts depends on how accurately they depict the kinds of human experiences being studied, what difference does it make whether the accounts are fictitious or actual happenings. I ask the question not to justify fiction but to pose a very important problem. The problem seems to be less a matter of the honesty of the informant and more a matter of accurate perceptiveness. This puts the problem in a markedly different light from that in which it is usually seen. It is clearly an unresolved methodological problem.

Testability

A major mark of a scientific instrument is that it yields data that can test and refute theoretical assertions made about the data. Scientific data must have a character which is independent of the theoretical interpretations made of the data; the data must be able to test whether the theoretical assertions fit. If the data give way to interpretations, supporting equally well diverse and contrary theoretical interpretations, the data must be seen as scientifically inadequate. This was found to be the case with much of the data given by the human documents used in *The Polish Peasant*. This, again, sets an important methodological problem—how can we get human documents to yield firm and decisive data?

One should be wary of simple schemes that are proposed as means of ensuring that the data given by human documents are firm and decisive. One scheme would be to limit the usable data in a document to those which are nailed down as items of established fact. Such a proposal would strip the human document of its most valuable content, since the primary information that is sought refers to how the given actor saw, defined, and handled situations; the accounts of these matters are seldom capable of being nailed down as established fact. Another scheme would be to ensure that the content of the document meets the criteria of representativeness, adequacy, and reliability that we have just been considering. This would obviously be splendid if it could be done; but as I hope I have shown in the preceding discussion, many methodological problems have to be overcome before these criteria, themselves, can be developed in the case of human documents. A third scheme would be to seek the given kinds of data that would resolve the conflict between divergent or contrary theoretical interpretations; logically, this is a very meritorious idea but one that is largely unworkable because of (1) now knowing what such missing data are and (2) not being able to secure the data. The unsatisfactory character of the three schemes that I have mentioned might seem to leave a bleak picture. Yet, there are procedures that offer the likelihood of firm and decisive data in the case of human documents. One is to use only those human documents which are known to come from informants who are knowledgeable about the given type of action under study. To ascertain who is knowledgeable and to gain, where needed, their cooperation are separate but manageable problems. An allied procedure to ensure that the data that one is using from human documents are firm and decisive is to subject the documents to rigorous examination and to collective dissection by a small group of such knowledgeable individuals. I will not spell out this latter technique. I merely wish to say that this technique, which is practically unknown to sociologists, is of inestimable value in separating valid data from spurious and questionable data. I make these few observations merely to suggest that the problem of getting firm and decisive data in the case of human documents is capable of being dealt with. The more important point to be stated here is that this methodological problem, so clearly posed by *The Polish Peasant*, has gained little attention from sociologists.

I wish to close this lengthy introduction by stressing that *The Polish Peasant* set a series of methodological problems of the gravest import to sociology. I have sought to identify these methodological problems in my present statement. These methodological problems remain even though sociologists in the pursuit of new interests are disposed to ignore them. The problems remain because they inevitably arise as soon as one recognizes that human beings in either their individual or collective capacity act by confronting and defining the situations in which their action takes place. The recognition forces scholars to bring "subjective" factors into consideration. Once this is done, the methodological problems have to be faced. Hopefully, the republication of my critique of *The Polish Peasant* may help to reawaken sociologists to a serious recognition of these methodological problems.

Berkeley, California

CONTENTS

FOREWORD

CURIOSITY has long been recognized as one of the great springs of human progress. It is our urge to find out that keeps our fund of useful knowledge constantly expanding. The more we learn, the more we itch to learn. It is an insatiable impulse—this curiosity.

It is also in part an indiscriminating impulse. It commonly derives from some specific motivation such as ambition, jealousy, admiration, affection, or pride. Clearly curiosity is frequently directed toward inconsequential things. The middle name of my grandfather on my mother's side may appear to me to be a bit of information much to be desired, but it is likely to prove of slight interest to anyone else and probably is of no particular consequence. The fact is that curiosity navigates the sea of the unknown with unrestricted fishing rights. The presumption seems to be that there is no means of telling when or where the catch will turn out to be useful.

Even when the catch is in hand, there is reluctance to conclude that some of it is not worth keeping. Who knows? Some day that apparently insignificant, if not worthless, bit of information may turn out to be a source of great illumination. So we proceed with the widest catholicity of interest and receptivity to gather information wherever it is to be had. The franchise of curiosity brooks no restrictions.

The situation is marked in certain areas by another important feature. Any acquisition of knowledge inevitably for the intelligent raises the question, "So what?" This is not an impertinent question. We speak of frontiers of knowledge.

The very concept of a frontier implies a territory behind the frontier in which effective organization prevails. With any accession of new information we are bound to ask: What is the bearing of this new information on the knowledge we have had? Does the new material add significantly to what we already knew?

For many large areas of knowledge the answers to these questions can be attempted only by those who belong to the select company of the expert. Is a given contribution relating to the life of a primitive people a truthful and significant addition to the sum total of human knowledge? Only a small company of recognized anthropologists are supposed to be able to say. The rest of the public must take the soundness and importance of the study largely on faith.

Under these circumstances what is to prevent the development of a self-contained and self-recruiting cult perpetuating inquiries and reports of no substantial social value, either in promise for the future or relevance for the present? The question becomes especially pertinent if the company of experts who are passing judgment on current investigations is being maintained, either directly or indirectly, at public expense.

The solution of the problem raised by this question would appear to lie in the acceptance by the experts of two fundamental propositions: First, inquiry in any field should recognize the necessity of continuous appraisal of the nature of the knowledge being acquired. Does it consist of the record of observed uniques the reappearance of which cannot be anticipated, or does it at least suggest generalizations which may be expected to illuminate and to some extent make more manageable later experience under similar circumstances? Is one of the primary purposes of inquiry to reach such generalizations, or is this a matter of indifference? Questions such as these should be answered by those in the particular field of investigation.

Second, the experts are under obligation to communicate to the public, in language the educated lay public can understand, the answers to questions such as those just stated. The lay public cannot be expected to follow the intricacies of technique necessary for practically all fields of specialized scholarly and scientific endeavor, but it can be led to understand the ends which are sought by the workers in a given field, as well as the nature of the results that are being obtained. The public is entitled to know on what basis the experts distinguish between success and failure, between the good and the bad, in their own work.

Some of this general line of thought came pointedly into the discussions of the Social Science Research Council at the annual conference of the Council in September, 1937. There was before the Council at the time the report of a Committee on Review of Council Policy. This committee had conducted a thoughtful examination of the Council's record from the very beginning of the Council in 1923. Certain conclusions had been reached by the Committee. The most sweeping of these was that the Council's interests and activities had veered too far toward the promotional and administrative and away from the critical and scientific. Excerpts from the Committee's findings read: "The first recommendation of the committee is that intellectual leadership in the facilitation and coordination of research in the social sciences be reasserted as the dominant and controlling purpose of the Council. . . . The Committee believes that during the course of the development of the Council the inevitable accumulation of legislative, administrative and fiscal interests, plus the increasing demands for service from governmental and other agencies, have gradually smothered or at least reduced the prominence of the intellectual function. . . . The Committee believes that action should be taken now looking toward a policy that places the heavier emphasis on the Council's efforts to put social research on a sounder scientific basis. . . . The Council can render its greatest service to society by exploring the fundamentals of social science." In conclusion the Committee proposed that the Council's future undertakings should be envisaged under four headings, including "appraisal."

Presentation of the report of the Committee of Review led the Council into an extended and at times highly animated discussion in which rather sharp differences of view among Council members were exposed. It became clear that certain members of the Council regarded any attempt by the Council to assess critically the work of social scientists as a well-nigh hopeless undertaking. Nevertheless at the conclusion of the debate the Council voted—

"That the Problems and Policy Committee be instructed to appoint a special committee with responsibility for planning such appraisals of completed research as in the judgment of the special committee shall discharge the Council's responsibility for the improvement of the quality of research in the social sciences."

The Committee on Appraisal of Research subsequently appointed by the Problems and Policy Committee consisted of Edmund E. Day, chairman, Francis W. Coker, Edwin G. Nourse, Albert T. Poffenberger, Robert Redfield, Arthur M. Schlesinger and Warren S. Thompson. This committee has since developed a program which has had the approval both of the Problems and Policy Committee and of the Council.

At the first meeting of the Appraisal Committee, on January 16, 1938, basic decisions were reached regarding the Committee's procedure. It was decided not to attempt any immediate formulation, however tentative, of criteria by which to judge of the value or significance of contributions in the social science field. Rather it was deemed advisable first to subject to critical analysis a selection of studies which were held in high regard by qualified specialists. Each member of the committee communicated with some twenty or thirty of the outstanding workers in the discipline of his special competence, both older men of established reputation and younger men of exceptional promise being included, asking each informant to submit a list of three to six works, published in the United States since the Great War, which in the informant's judgment had made the most significant contributions to knowledge in the particular discipline—economics, or anthropology, or whatever the discipline might be—with regard to which the informant was presumably qualified to speak. In asking the informant for these lists of most significant contributions, the committee explicitly stated its unwillingness to set up any criteria of significance. The whole idea at this point was to get from the disciplinary specialists themselves a certified list of contributions thought by the specialists to have high value. Close examination of these selected works might then throw light on the nature of significance in social science research.

As might have been expected, the returns of the informants exhibited a good deal of scattering, but they left no doubt that certain books in each field were held in high repute. From these the committee made a selection of six to be subjected to critical appraisal. The six so selected were:

Berle and Means	*Modern Corporations*
Boas	*Primitive Art*
Dickinson	*Administrative Justice*
Mills	*Behavior of Prices*
Thomas and Znaniecki	*The Polish Peasant in Europe and America*
Webb	*The Great Plains*

The next step by the committee was to secure competent assessors of these six outstanding works. It was expected by the committee that an adequate critique, even by a competent scholar thoroughly familiar with the publication, would take several weeks of intensive application. Each appraisal was to bring out as far as possible: the purpose of the author in making the study; the degree of success of the author in achieving this purpose; any observations or generalizations reached in the study, and the extent to which they appeared to rest firmly upon the materials presented. Modest honoraria were offered to those invited to undertake the work. The response of those solicited was unexpectedly favorable. Apparently the nature of the assignment was intriguing. The cooperation of an excellent group of appraisers was promptly secured.

One of the first of the critiques to be completed was that of Thomas and Znaniecki's *The Polish Peasant* done by Professor Herbert Blumer of the Department of Sociology of the University of Chicago. It is the Appraisal Committee's opinion that Blumer's critique is a highly illuminating analysis of a most important publication. The committee had no hesitation in transmitting the appraisal, with an explanation of the committee's purposes and procedures, to one of the co-authors of *The Polish Peasant,* W. I. Thomas. The result was a rejoinder, written in admirable spirit, which throws further light upon the conditions under which the study of the Polish peasant was made, and the purposes the study was designed to serve. Mr. Znaniecki was abroad during the year, but has contributed his comment.

The Blumer critique and the Thomas rejoinder were made the subject matter of a special conference held under the sponsorship of the Appraisal Committee at the Council offices on December 10, 1938. In addition to Thomas and

Professor Blumer, eleven social scientists who were known to be interested in some of the questions raised by the Blumer appraisal were invited to participate. Four members of the Appraisal Committee attended as auditors. The all-day conference discussion ranged widely over questions of method and result in social science research, and further light was thrown on the nature of the contributions made by Thomas and Znaniecki when they published their monumental work.

The Blumer critique, the Thomas rejoinder, the conference digest, and comments by Znaniecki, and conference members, have been thought by the Appraisal Committee worthy of publication. The Committee expects in time to present similar analyses of other outstanding works in the social science field. It is hoped in this way to contribute to a growing interest among social scientists in the nature of insight and proof in the interpretation of social phenomena. The nature of social knowledge is a fundamental problem which social science must squarely face. Only so can we hope to advance steadily in our understanding of the infinitely complex human relationships which we so glibly subsume under the term society. Only so can we in time get social science to contribute effectively to the more intelligent direction of human affairs.

EDMUND E. DAY

July 30, 1939

Part One

ANALYSIS
by
Herbert Blumer
of
The Polish Peasant in Europe and America
by
W. I. Thomas and Florian Znaniecki

Part One

Blumer's Analysis

CHARACTER AND PURPOSE OF THE WORK

The Polish Peasant in Europe and America, by W. I. Thomas and Florian Znaniecki, is a five volume work published during the years 1918-1920.[1] It is a result of several years of investigation made by the authors. They describe their work as follows:

> The work consists of five volumes, largely documentary in their character. Volumes I and II comprise a study of the organization of the peasant primary groups (family and community), and of the partial evolution of this system of organization under the influence of the new industrial system and of immigration to America and Germany. Volume III is the autobiography (with critical treatment) of an immigrant of peasant origin but belonging by occupation to the lower city class, and illustrates the tendency to disorganization of the individual under the conditions involved in a rapid transition from one type of social organization to another. Volume IV treats the dissolution of the primary group and the social and political reorganization and unification of peasant communities in Poland on the new ground of rational cooperation. Volume V is based on studies of the Polish immigrant in America and shows the degrees and forms of disorganization associated with a too-rapid and inadequately mediated individualization, with a sketch of the beginnings of reorganization.[2]

[1] The work was republished in 1927 in a two volume edition without change except a different ordering of the parts and different pagination. References are to this later edition.

Some of the outstanding reviews of *The Polish Peasant* are: *Am. J. Sociol.,* 848 ff., May 1918, Albion W. Small; *ibid.,* 331 ff., Nov. 1918, H. P. Fairchild; *ibid.,* 816 ff., March 1928, Ellsworth Faris; *Nation,* 301 ff., March 14, 1928, Solomon Bluhm; *Survey,* 166 ff., May 11, 1918, E. G. Balch; *ibid.,* 559 ff., Sept. 1, 1928, Louis Wirth.

[2] Vol. I, viii

This short statement might suggest that the work is just a monograph on Polish peasant life under the conditions which they specify. It is this, to be sure, but it is also infinitely more than this. The work is actually a broadside treatment of the theoretical problems set by the study of contemporary social life. It is clear that the authors view Polish peasant life as undergoing extensive social change and, further, that they regard this social change as generically similar to that of our contemporary social life.

> Our civilization, when taken not only in its highest manifestations but in its totality, is still in the midst of the same process of change which began a half century ago among the Polish peasants.[3]

What they propose in their treatment of Polish peasant life is actually a scheme for the study and analysis of contemporary society. This is indicated by the first two paragraphs of the preface:

> Among the questions included in the as yet relatively unformulated field of social science (without reference to logical order) are: immigration; racial prejudice; cultural assimilation; the comparative mental and moral worth of races and nationalities; crime, alcoholism, vagabondage, and other forms of anti-social behavior; nationalism and internationalism; democracy and class-hierarchization; efficiency and happiness, particularly as functions of the relation of the individual to the social framework containing his activities; the rate of individualization possible without disorganization; the difference between unreflective social cohesion brought about by tradition, and reflective cooperation brought about by rational selection of common ends and means; the introduction of new and desirable attitudes and values without recourse to the way of revolution; and, more generally, the determination of the most general and particular laws of social reality, preliminary to the introduction of a social control as satisfactory, or as increasingly satisfactory, as is our control of the material world, resulting from the study of the laws of physical reality.
>
> Now we are ourselves primarily interested in these problems, but we are convinced of the necessity of approaching these and other social problems by isolating given societies and studying them, first in the totality of their objective complexity, and then comparatively. The present study

[3] Vol. II, 1118-19

was not, in fact, undertaken exclusively or even primarily as an expression of interest in the Polish peasant (although our selection of this society was influenced by the question of immigration and by other considerations), but the Polish peasant was selected rather as a convenient object for the exemplification of a standpoint and method outlined in the methodological note forming the first pages of the present volume. The scope of our study will be best appreciated by having this fact in mind.[4]

The large number of problems indicated in the first paragraph show the diversity of interests which the authors have had in approaching their study. Their belief that the change taking place in Polish peasant life is common with that in contemporary social life suggests the need of an extensive theoretical scheme for the discussion of social change. Their last quoted remark that their study exemplifies a "standpoint and method" suggests further their work is more than a mere monograph on the Polish peasant.

Indeed, their undertaking has led them to propose an extensive outline of a "methodology" essential to the study of social life; and to develop an extensive social theory, primarily in the form of a system of social psychology and in the essentials of a sociology. This has involved an extensive statement of the premises of social research; the development of a number of new techniques of social research, the extensive use of "human" documents as a new source of data for research, the development of a full "framework of reference," including a significant number of new concepts; as well as the formulation of a series of new theories, such as those of personal and social disorganization, and of the nature and development of personality.

Any one of these undertakings would have gained for the work a place of conspicuous importance; their totality explains the usual characterization of the work as "monumental." The

[4] Vol. I, vii, viii

work has exercised a profound influence: in orienting social research among sociologists; in introducing new techniques of research, such as the life history; in imparting to sociology a social psychological slant; in introducing a number of concepts, now widely used, such as "social attitude," "definition of the situation," and the "four wishes;" and in contributing new theories to sociological knowledge.

Because of the vastness of the work (the two volume edition runs close to 2250 pages) and because of the wealth and variety of interests developed, the task of critically appraising it is not easy or simple. The treatment given in this paper will endeavor to cut through the complexity and profuseness of the discussion, and to cling closely to the "standpoint and method" and its application. It is the explication and exemplification of this "standpoint and method" which is the avowed purpose of the work and which forms its major theme. The consideration of the standpoint and method will lead us to postpone a discussion of the monographic phase of the work, and subsequently when considering it, to limit the treatment to what is essential to an understanding and evaluation of the standpoint and method. It should be mentioned here, consequently, that there is in the work a wealth of depiction and analysis of Polish peasant life which are worthy of the highest respect but which have no place in this analysis.

METHODOLOGY

Since the authors have declared their study to be an exemplification of a standpoint and of a method, it is essential to make clear their methodological position. In their discussion, they are proposing a scheme which they regard as the indispensable premise for *the scientific study of social life,* and for the development of *a scientific social theory.*

It is advisable to understand again that the authors are interested in an approach that will be suited to the study of "actual civilized society in its full development and with all its complexity." Such a society is marked primarily by change, due in large measure to the increased rapidity of social evolution, to the breakdown of the isolation of groups, and to the appearance of more frequent and varied crises. This character of *change* looms up as centrally important, and must be caught by any scheme adequate to the study of contemporary life. An adequate social theory must be able to cope with the problem of social control as it is set by such changing social life.

A method which permits us to determine only cases of stereotyped activity and leaves us helpless in face of changed conditions is not a scientific method at all, and becomes even less and less practically useful with the continual increase of fluidity in modern social life.[5]

The method to be employed in the study of social life, consequently, must permit one to establish relations between the essential factors involved in social change. These relations must be causal and must apply to the process of change, or as the authors call it, the process of *becoming*.

The chief problems of modern science are problems of causal explanation. The determination and systematization of data is only the first step in scientific investigation. If science wishes to lay the foundations of a technique, it must attempt to understand and to control the process of *becoming*. Social theory cannot avoid this task, and there is only one way of fulfilling it. Social becoming, like natural becoming, must be analyzed into a plurality of facts, each of which represents a succession of cause and effect. The idea of social theory is the analysis of the totality of social becoming into such causal processes and a systematization permitting us to understand the connections between these processes.[6]

As the above quotation indicates, the first step in this undertaking is the "determination of data." One has to resolve social becoming into primary or basic factors between which one can ascertain cause and effect relations. This, the authors

[5] Vol. I, 43   [6] Vol. I, 36

have done. They declare that "attitudes" and "values" are the basic data of social becoming.

It is necessary to make this clear; for these two terms and the relation between them constitute the foundation for their whole scheme and undertaking. The cue to the nature of these primary data of social life is provided by two fundamental practical problems. "These are (1) the problem of the dependence of the individual upon social organization and culture, and (2) the problem of the dependence of social organization and culture upon the individual." The individual and social organization are the factors of group life; the basic data, consequently, must refer to these two factors.

If social theory is to become the basis of social technique and to solve these problems really, it is evident that it must include both kinds of data involved in them—namely, the objective cultural elements of social life and the subjective characteristics of the members of the social group —and that the two kinds of data must be taken as correlated. For these data we shall use now and in the future the terms 'social values' (or simply 'values') and 'attitudes.'[7]

This identification of values with "the objective cultural elements of social life," and of attitudes with "the subjective characteristics" of the individual is made clearer by their formal definitions:

By a social value we understand any datum having an empirical content accessible to the members of some social group and a meaning with regard to which it is or may be an object of activity. Thus, a foodstuff, an instrument, a coin, a piece of poetry, a university, a myth, a scientific theory, are social values. Each of them has a content that is sensual in the case of foodstuff, the instrument, the coin; partly sensual, partly imaginary in the piece of poetry, whose content is constituted, not only by the written or spoken words, but also by the images which they evoke, and in the case of the university, whose content is the whole complex of men, buildings, material accessories, and images representing its activity; or, finally, only imaginary in the case of a mythical personality or a scientific theory. The meaning of these values becomes explicit when we

[7] Vol. I, 20-21

take them in connection with human actions. The meaning of the food-stuff is its reference to its eventual consumption; that of an instrument, its reference to the work for which it is designed; that of a coin, the possibilities of buying and selling or the pleasures of spending which it involves; that of the piece of poetry, the sentimental and intellectual re-actions which it arouses; that of the university, the social activities which it performs; that of the mythical personality, the cult of which it is the object and the actions of which it is supposed to be the author; that of the scientific theory, the possibilities of control of experience by idea or action that it permits.[8]

By attitude we understand a process of individual consciousness which determines real or possible activity of the individual in the social world. Thus, hunger that compels the consumption of the foodstuff; the work-man's decision to use the tool; the tendency of the spendthrift to spend the coin; the poet's feelings and ideas expressed in the poem and the reader's sympathy and admiration; the needs which the institution tries to satisfy and the response it provokes; the fear and devotion manifested in the cult of the divinity; the interest in creating, understanding, or applying a scientific theory and the ways of thinking implied in it—all these are attitudes. The attitude is thus the individual counterpart of the social value; activity, in whatever form, is the bond between them.[9]

Later, we shall consider more fully the nature of attitudes and values. Here, it is sufficient to understand that the authors regard them as the basic theoretical units into which social life can be resolved. It is in their relations that one must seek the causal processes into which "social becoming" is to be analyzed. Change in social life, in other words, is to be ac-counted for in terms of the interaction of attitudes and values.

The authors have expressed this view in their central methodological formula:

The fundamental methodological principle of both social psychology and sociology—the principle without which they can never reach scientific explanation—is therefore the following one: *The cause of a social or individual phenomenon is never another social or individual phe-nomenon alone, but always a combination of a social and an indi-vidual phenomenon. Or, in more exact terms: The cause of a value or of an attitude is never an attitude or a value alone, but always a combination of an attitude and a value.*[10]

[8] Vol. I, 21   [9] Vol. I, 22   [10] Vol. I, 44

It is necessary to explain this view, the adoption of which the authors declare to be essential to the foundation of adequate social theory. This explanation is made easier by considering the methodological weakness of social practice and social theory which fail to take into account both subjective and objective factors. Most social practice and theory show this weakness in being based on the assumption of "identical reactions to identical influences."

These assumptions are: (1) that men react in the same way to the same influences regardless of their individual or social past, and that therefore it is possible to provoke identical behavior in various individuals by identical means; (2) that men develop spontaneously, without external influence, tendencies which enable them to profit in a full and uniform way from given conditions, and that therefore it is sufficient to create favorable or remove unfavorable conditions in order to give birth to or suppress given tendencies.[11]

These assumptions, the authors declare, are shown particularly in the fields of social reform, education, and law, as far as social practice is concerned, and in much of social science as far as social theory is concerned. They remark:

The assumption of the spontaneous development of tendencies if the material conditions are given is found in the exaggerted importance ascribed by social reformers to changes of material environment and in the easy conclusions drawn from material conditions on the mentality and character of individuals and groups. For example, it is assumed that good housing conditions will create a good family life, that the abolition of saloons will stop drinking, that the organization of a well-endowed institution is all that is necessary to make the public realize its value in practice.[12]
. . . the wrong formula has been used very thoroughly and has led to such imposing systems as, in reflective practice, the whole enormous and continually growing complexity of positive law, and in social theory to the more recent and limited, but rapidly growing, accumulation of works on political science, philosophy of law, ethics, and sociology.[13]

The whole position of the authors on this important point is given in the following lengthy statement:

[11] Vol. I, 12   [12] Vol. I, 13   [13] Vol. I, 52

. . . the chief error of both social practice and social theory has been that they determined, consciously or unconsciously, social facts in a way which excluded in advance the possibility of their subordination to any laws. The implicit or explicit assumption was that a social fact is composed of two elements, a cause which is either a social phenomenon or an individual act, and an effect which is either an individual act or a social phenomenon. Following uncritically the example of the physical sciences, which always tend to find the one determined phenomenon which is the necessary and sufficient condition of another phenomenon, social theory and social practice have forgotten to take into account one essential difference between physical and social reality, which is that, while the effect of a physical phenomenon depends exclusively on the objective nature of this phenomenon and can be calculated on the ground of the latter's empirical content, the effect of a social phenomenon depends in addition on the subjective standpoint taken by the individual or the group toward this phenomenon and can be calculated only if we know, not only the objective content of the assumed cause, but also the meaning which it has at the given moment for the given conscious beings. This simple consideration should have shown to the social theorist or technician that a social cause cannot be simple, like a physical cause, but is compound, and must include both an objective and a subjective element, a value *and* an attitude.[14]

In fact, a social value, acting upon individual members of the group, produces a more or less different effect on every one of them; even when acting upon the same individual at various moments it does not influence him uniformly.[15]

If we wish to explain the appearance of a new attitude—whether in one individual or in a whole group—we know that this attitude appeared as a consequence of the influence of a social value upon the individual or the group, but we know also that this influence itself would have been impossible unless there had been some pre-existing attitude, some wish, emotional habit, or intellectual tendency, to which this value has in some way appealed, favoring it, contradicting it, giving it a new direction, or stabilizing its hesitating expressions. Our problem is therefore to find both the value and the pre-existing attitude upon which it has acted and get in their combination the necessary and sufficient cause of the new attitude.[16]

These various quotations make clear the contention of the authors that the deficiency of social theory and practice has been the failure to realize the presence of both individual and social components in social situations. In social life, external

[14] Vol. I, 38   [15] Vol. I, 39   [16] Vol. I, 44, 45

or objective factors are playing upon individuals, and through the medium of the experience of these individuals, lead to given forms of human conduct. Accordingly, it is necessary to consider the subjective dispositions of individuals that determine how they will respond to the objective factor playing upon them. It is in this relation between objective factors and subjective dispositions, which Thomas and Znaniecki call respectively value and attitude, that causal sequences are to be sought. An attitude can change only as a result of an outside value acting on it; a value can change only as a result of an attitude acting on it. If one can designate the specific value acting on an identifiable attitude and isolate the resulting attitude, or if one can mark the attitude playing on a given value and determine the resulting value, one has isolated in either instance a law of social becoming. A few illustrations proposed by the authors at different points may be given here to clarify their conception and illustrate "laws of becoming."

1. Thus two individuals under the influence of tyrannical behavior of their father may react differently; one is submissive and the other rebellious. This is due to the fact that the first has a strong attitude of family solidarity; the other a strong individualistic attitude to assert his own personal desires. This suggests two laws of social becoming: (1) a value in the form of parental tyranny playing on an attitude of family solidarity gives rise to an attitude of submissiveness; (2) the same value playing on an attitude of self-assertion leads to an attitude of revolt.

2. The history of Polish peasants shows the existence among them of an economic organization which is distinctly familial in character marked by the common sharing of economic values. In recent years this has been succeeded by 'an individualistic system with a quantification of the values.' The attitude involved in the formation of this new social value is the tendency to economic advance. Thus we obtain the formula: 'familial system—tendency to advance—individualistic system.'

3. Among the Poles it has been observed that frequently in the case of a lawsuit false testimony is given by witnesses on both sides despite the oath. This seems to be due to the fact that Polish peasants 'bring into court a fighting attitude.' Thus there is suggested the following sociological law: "the lawsuit and a radical fighting attitude result in false testimonies."

[12]

These illustrations indicate the nature of the causal relations which the authors believe may be reached through the application of the methodological principle. The ideal objective of scientific research is to ascertain such "laws of becoming," which can be systematized into a body of social theory.

It should be noted here that their methodological conception of the relation between subjective and objective factors can be viewed in two ways. One is a general way, amounting merely to the recognition that the influence of either factor is dependent on the nature of the other. The other is a specific way, implying the existence of precise and invariable relations between attitudes and values which can be expressed in definite laws of social becoming. The latter represents, perhaps, the ideal and ultimate objective. As we shall see, the authors actually operate with the first of these ways and do not use the latter.

In seeking to establish a relation between given attitudes and values, the authors stress that three considerations must be observed. First, the comparative method should be employed in arriving at a law or relation; one should compare many instances of the given attitude and value to determine the relation between them. Second, in this endeavor it is very important not to wrench the attitude and value out of their context. One must take "into account the whole life of a given society instead of arbitrarily selecting and isolating beforehand certain particular groups of facts.[17] "Third, when a presumed generalization has been established, the hypothesis cannot be regarded as fully tested until the scientist has made a "systematic search for such experiences as may contradict it, and proved those contradictions to be only seeming, explicable by the interference of definite factors."[18] Since social theory,

[17] Vol. I, 18
[18] Vol. I, 65

strictly speaking, is not subject to experimental tests, the scientist should make an active search for negative cases.

These three points are of considerable importance. With reference to the first, it should be noted that Thomas and Znaniecki emphasize repeatedly the need of comparative studies, especially between different societies; indeed, the scheme which they are proposing in *The Polish Peasant* is offered as one to be tested on other groups. Concerning the second point, they are insistent again on the need of taking a society in its totality, if one wishes to avoid fallacious interpretations arising from restricted and piece-meal studies. The third point is merely a valuable caution designed to compensate for the fact that the experimental method, rigidly conceived, cannot be employed in the study of social life.

The development of a body of social theory consisting of such secure and objective knowledge of the relations between attitudes and values would provide the basis for adequate social control. Thomas and Znaniecki ever have in mind the formulation of social theory that is derived from, and that applies to, the actual process of change or becoming as it occurs in contemporary social life. While it is distinctly advisable that social research be free from too immediate reference to practical aims, nevertheless, the test of science is "ultimate practical applicability." Social theory in the form of laws of social becoming will be adequate for social control.

The authors recognize a difficulty, however, in the application of scientific laws. Such laws are abstract and the practical situations are concrete. In social practice, the elements which we want to use or modify are always embodied in situations with which our activity must comply. Whether one wishes to modify individual attitudes or social institutions, one must take into account the nature of the situation. The situation involves three kinds of data:

(1) The objective conditions under which the individual or society has to act, that is, the totality of values—economic, social, religious, intellectual, etc.—which at the given moment affect directly or indirectly the conscious status of the individual or the group. (2) The pre-existing attitudes of the individual or the group which at the given moment have an actual influence upon his behavior. (3) The definition of the situation, that is, the more or less clear conception of the conditions and consciousness of the attitudes.[19]

The situation can evidently be controlled either by a change of conditions or by a change of attitudes, or by both, and in this respect the rôle of technique as application of science is easily characterized. By comparing situations of a certain type, the social technician must find what are the predominant values or the predominant attitudes which determine the situation more than others, and then the question is to modify these values or these attitudes in the desired way by using the knowledge of social causation given by social theory.[20]

One other point should be mentioned here that is important to the problem of social control. This point, as we shall see later, is also a significant item in the scheme of social theory which the authors develop. The point can be best given in their own words:

We have assumed throughout this argument that if an adequate technique is developed it is possible to produce any desirable attitudes and values, but this assumption is practically justified only if we find in the individual attitudes which cannot avoid response to the class of stimulations which society is able to apply to him. And apparently we do find this disposition. Every individual has a vast variety of wishes which can be satisfied only by his incorporation in a society. Among his general patterns of wishes we may enumerate: (1) the desire for new experience, for fresh stimulations; (2) the desire for recognition, including, for example, sexual response and general social appreciation, and secured by devices ranging from the display of ornament to the demonstration of worth through scientific attainment; (3) the desire for mastery, or the "will to power," exemplified by ownership, domestic tyranny, political despotism, based on the instinct of hate, but capable of being sublimated to laudable ambition; (4) the desire for security, based on the instinct of fear and exemplified negatively by the wretchedness of the individual in perpetual solitude or under social taboo. Society is, indeed, an agent for the repression of many of the wishes in the individual; it demands that he shall be moral by repressing at least the wishes which are irreconcilable with the welfare of the group, but

[19] Vol. I, 68   [20] Vol. I, 70

nevertheless it provides the only medium within which any of his schemes or wishes can be gratified. And it would be superfluous to point out by examples the degree to which society has in the past been able to impose its schemes of attitudes and values on the individual. . . . And even if we find that the attitudes are not so tractable as we have assumed, that it is not possible to provoke all the desirable ones, we shall still be in the same situation as, let us say, physics and mechanics: we shall have the problem of securing the highest degree of control possible in view of the nature of our materials.[21]

The view presented in these remarks is that the four wishes of which the authors speak are basic attitudes which can be used for the formation of new desired attitudes through the application of the proper social values. Since these attitudes are present in all human beings and require some form of satisfaction, they can always be appealed to or played upon. Consequently, if one desires to develop in individuals certain specific attitudes, one may use these fundamental wishes as the basis, by applying to them the appropriate values in accordance with established laws of social becoming.

What we have said so far concerning the authors' central methodological view should not only make clear its character, but indicate why Thomas and Znaniecki regard its application as the essential aim of scientific social research and why they view it as the only means of securing a social theory adequate for social control. Accordingly, they believe that it is a guiding scheme which social science must follow in its scientific undertakings.

One should note here that the knowledge which this methodological procedure would yield would be different from and more adequate than forms of social knowledge which are now sought in contemporary social research. At different places in their discussion, the authors refer to several of these types of knowledge which are regarded by their respective adherents as "scientific" and as the proper kind of knowledge

[21] Vol. I, 72-74

which social science should seek. It is appropriate here to list several that are currently popular, and show how they are regarded by Thomas and Znaniecki.

1. One of the most frequent types is that which consists of "common sense" generalization. With reference to this kind of knowledge, the authors remark ". . . all the generalizations constituting the common sense social theory and based on individual experience are both insignificant and subject to innumerable exceptions."[22] Such knowledge is arrived at without method and is dependent on mere individual experience and judgment. Because of these deficiencies little hope can be entertained for scientific knowledge as long as one continues to rely on common sense procedure. It is gratuitous to point out that a great deal of contemporary social theory is of this kind; and that the authors desire a methodological framework which will escape, and rise above, the limitations of common sense theory.

2. A second type of knowledge which one finds in contemporary social science, consists of scattered generalizations and usually minute "findings" that come from what the authors term "planless empiricism." By planless empiricism, they refer to "trying to get at the real cause by a rather haphazard selection of various possibilities." Undoubtedly a great deal of contemporary social research is of this sort—operating without any fundamental theoretical guidance, but claiming justification on the ground of its objectivity. Thomas and Znaniecki clearly regard this form of research and its resulting knowledge as highly inadequate and methodologically deficient. This is why, as we shall see, they give to their own study an extensive and careful theoretical guidance.

3. A third type of social knowledge consists of mere statements of uniformities of social behavior in response to social influences. This kind of knowledge is particularly likely to come from social research which confines itself to "objective" or external facts. It is very extensive today because of the popularity of this form of social research. With respect to it, the authors state:
". . . such uniformities of reaction to social influences as can be found constitute a problem in themselves. . . If the members of a certain group react in an identical way to certain values, it is because they have been socially trained to react thus . . . we cannot assume that this value alone is the cause of this reaction."[23]

Their general reaction against this type of knowledge is indicated by the following passage:
. . . social science cannot remain on the surface of social becoming where certain schools wish to have it float, but must reach the actual

[22] Vol. I, 7   [23] Vol. I, 40-41

human experiences and attitudes which constitute the full, live, and active social reality beneath the formal organization of social institutions, or behind the statistically tabulated mass-phenomena which taken in themselves are nothing but symptoms of unknown causal processes and can serve only as provisional ground for sociological hypotheses.[24]

4. A fourth type of knowledge widely current in present day social science consists of

statements of causal influences which hold true 'on the average,' 'in the majority of cases.' This is a flat self-contradiction, for, if something *is a cause,* it must by its very definition, always and necessarily have *the same effect,* otherwise it is not a cause at all."[25]

The authors aspire to knowledge which is genuinely causal.

5. A fifth kind of knowledge results from the effort to resolve what must be taken as a primary relation into simpler elements. In doing so, the analysis is pushed below and away from the character of the data in which one is interested and this character and the value of the data are lost. Such types of study represent an unnecessary and misleading analysis and indicate a misunderstanding of the locus of the complexity which it is felt must be resolved. The authors refer to this type of study as attempts

"to analyze phenomena acting upon individuals and individual reactions to them into simpler elements, hoping thus to find simple facts, while the trouble is not with the complexity of the data but with the complexity of the context on which these data act or in which they are embodied . . ."[26]

These kinds of knowledge are regarded by the authors as deficient. They believe their own methodological scheme provides the approach necessary for securing knowledge which is genuinely scientific.

It is of importance in this analysis of Thomas and Znaniecki's work to note that they have not given any "laws of social becoming" that stand the test of their own specified requirements, such as that of making a conscientious search for negative instances. In fact, it must be pointed out that there is a marked paucity, even, of *proposed* laws, despite the fact that, as we shall see, they are working with an abundance

[24] Vol. II, 1834   [25] Vol. I, 39   [26] Vol. I, 39-40

of material and that they make generalizations very freely. Only on rare occasions do they suggest possible laws; some of these are frankly speculative and given merely for the purpose of illustration, and others are stated very tentatively.

Some explanation of this absence of laws of social becoming is given by statements in which the authors assert or imply that they did not seek to determine such laws. Thus, they declare that such laws "can be attained only by a long and persistent cooperation of social theoricians." Again, they remark that their "purpose is to give an insight into the mechanism of the research" necessary to arrive at such laws; and, further, they state that their work "evidently cannot in any sense pretend to establish social theory on a definitely scientific basis." "Our present very limited task is the preparation of a certain body of materials, even if we occasionally go beyond it and attempt to reach some generalization."[27] Despite these explanations, it is fitting to inquire further as to the reason for the absence of established laws of social becoming. Such inquiry will permit us to judge the validity of the methodological principle and to assess its value. To do this, however, it is necessary first to take up for consideration the framework which the authors propose for social theory, for this framework is an essential portion of their methodological position.

A summary paragraph here may be of help. Thomas and Znaniecki are desirous of making a *scientific* analysis of Polish peasant society. Consequently, they seek to employ an approach which will be suited to the study of group life under all conditions. This leads them to propose a methodological scheme which they regard as the foundation for social research and for social theory. Such a scheme must be suited to what is intrinsic and peculiar to human groups. As such, it must meet two facts: the changing character of contemporary social life;

[27] Vol. I, 74

and the subjective character of human experience. To meet the first fact, the scheme must resolve social happening into causal relations which ultimately will enable social control. To meet the second fact, the scheme must catch the subjective dispositions and interpretations in terms of which human beings react to external influences. The scheme proposed by the authors resolves social happening into an interaction of attitudes and values, which stand, respectively, for subjective dispositions and objective influences. The task of social research is to identify attitudes and values, to ascertain their interaction, and to isolate the causal relations between them. The resulting knowledge is recognized as being superior to current types of knowledge which are not adapted to the fact of social change, which ignore the subjective factor, which are based on "common sense," are in the form of "planless empiricism," which do not seek genuine causal relations, and which reduce the subjective and objective factors to simpler terms that do not retain what is peculiar to human behavior.

FRAMEWORK OF SOCIAL THEORY

The work of Thomas and Znaniecki is notable for the schemes of social psychology and sociology which the authors propose. Together, these constitute what they regard as social theory. Their views in this respect are woven into the "standpoint and method" which their extensive study of Polish peasant life is to illustrate. The "units" of the social theory are attitudes and values, as defined previously.

An attitude, as the authors state, is "a process of individual consciousness which determines real or possible activity of the individual in the social world." The two key terms here are "process of consciousness" and "activity." The first makes clear that an attitude, as conceived by the authors, may refer to any manifestation of conscious life. It may be an appetite, a habit, an impulse, a biological need, a feeling, an emotion, an interest, an idea, a decision, and so forth:

> . . . *every manifestation of conscious life* (my italics), however simple or complex, general or particular, can be treated as an attitude . . .[28]

"Attitudes" become, seemingly, blanket terms for all phases of mental life or psychological processes. Indeed, this is what the authors declare:

> . . . we may continue to use for different classes of attitudes the same terms which individual psychology has used for psychological processes, since these terms constitute the common property of all reflection about conscious life."[29]

In view of this identification of attitudes with psychological processes, one may ask if the authors are not merely borrowing the content of psychology and incorporating it into their social theory. The answer is emphatically in the negative. They take pains to stress that there is a significant difference between a psychological process considered in terms of itself and such a process as a tendency to act toward some value or object. In the first instance, it is a "psychical state"; in the second, an "attitude." "The psychological process remains always fundamentally *a state of somebody;* the attitude always fundamentally an *attitude toward something.*"[30] Psychology, as traditionally conceived, studies the nature of psychic states or psychological processes and attempts to establish the relations between them.

When one, however, studies these psychological processes in terms of their implied activity toward some object, one is undertaking a different task, and correspondingly one's methods will be entirely different. This task delimits the field of social psychology; "social psychology is precisely the science of attitudes." Since an attitude is always an actual or implied

[28] Vol. I, 27   [29] Vol. I, 23   [30] Vol. I, 23

tendency to act and has reference always to some value, or objective phase of social life, it can be thought of as a process of consciousness "as manifested in culture." Thus, the authors are led to refer to social psychology as a "general science of the subjective side of social culture."[31]

While, theoretically, social psychology includes the study of all attitudes, practically, the authors declare, its field consists primarily of

all the attitudes which are more or less generally found among the members of a social group, have a real importance in the life-organization of the individuals who have developed them, and manifest themselves in social activities of these individuals.[32]

Just as the authors set up social psychology on the basis of "attitudes," so, in a comparable way, they conceive of sociology as centering around the concept of "social value." The similarity, however, is not identical, since a certain kind of social value is singled out as the concern of sociology. This type of value is spoken of as "a rule."

As a previous quotation has shown, Thomas and Znaniecki regard a value as "any datum having an empirical content accessible to the members of some social group and a meaning with regard to which it is or may be an object of activity." The key terms here are "content" and "meaning." The content may be sensory, as in the case of a material object, or imaginary, as in the case of a "mythical personality." The meaning contained in the value consists of the social function of the value, i.e., the use to which it is put by people or the reactions which it arouses on their part—"The meaning of the foodstuff is its reference to its eventual consumption; that of an instrument, its reference to the work for which it is designed." A "natural thing" may have a content, but until it acquires a meaning, it is valueless. Finally, a social value may have many

[31] Vol. I, 31   [32] Vol. I, 30

meanings, for it may refer to many different kinds of activity.

With this reminder of the nature of social values as conceived by the authors, we may take up the nature of the specific kind of values referred to as rules. These values consist of the

more or less explicit and formal *rules* of behavior by which the group tends to maintain, to regulate, and to make more general and more frequent the corresponding type of actions among its members. These rules . . . (are in the nature of) . . . customs and rituals, legal and educational norms, obligatory beliefs and aims, etc. . . .[33]

Toward such rules, individuals may bring to bear different attitudes, such as those of appreciation or depreciation, a desire for personal freedom, or a feeling of social righteousness; hence, these rules are legitimately social values. They have "for every individual a certain content and a certain meaning." As social values, these rules exist alongside of other bodies of objective cultural data which may be the object matter of other cultural sciences like economics, philology, etc.

It is out of such rules that social institutions and the social organization are constituted.

The rules of behavior, and the actions viewed as conforming or not conforming with these rules, constitute with regard to their objective significance a certain number of more or less connected and harmonious systems which can be generally called *social institutions,* and the totality of institutions found in a concrete social group constitutes the *social organization* of this group.[34]

Sociology thus becomes the study of social organization. Social psychology is essentially the study of the subjective side of this social organization. Together they constitute social theory.

. . . both social psychology and sociology can be embraced under the general term of social theory, as they are both concerned with the relation between the individual and the concrete social group, though their standpoints on this common ground are quite opposite, and though their fields are not equally wide, social psychology comprising the attitudes of the individual toward *all* cultural values of the given social group, while sociology can study only one type of these values—social rules— in their relation to individual attitudes.[35]

In these remarks, we have the essentials of the framework for social theory. One may regard social life in two ways: objectively and subjectively. Viewed objectively, it presents itself as an organization made up of social rules. The study of this organization is the task of sociology; the primary problem is that of change in this organization; this is the result of new attitudes playing upon the old organization. Viewed subjectively, social life consists of attitudes held by individuals primarily in relation to the social organization; again the central problem is that of change; and this occurs through the operation of new values. The task of sociology is to study the social organization and to observe how it changes under the influence of new attitudes; the task of social psychology is to study attitudes and to observe how they change under the influence of values.

It is clear from the discussion that the scheme of social theory and the methodological conception are interwoven. Together, they constitute what the authors have called their "standpoint and method." It is now appropriate to consider this position critically.

CRITICISM OF THE METHODOLOGICAL POSITION

The immediate discussion that follows is primarily of a logical character. Let us point out, first of all, that the basic terms "attitude" and "value" as employed by Thomas and Znaniecki are vague, ambiguous, and confused. "Attitude" becomes a kind of psychological catchall, since, as the authors

[35] Vol. I, 33

[24]

state, it may refer to any psychological process, or item of consciousness. To take as a basic datum anything that includes such diverse things as appetites, conceptions, feelings, decisions, sensations, desires, ideas, and sentiments, is to operate with a complicated and indefinite concept. Vagueness of a similar sort seems to mark a "social value."

The imprecision and ambiguity is reflected in the confusion *between* the two terms as they are employed by the authors in their analyses. Frequently, the authors refer to essentially the same thing by either attitude or value; in other places, either term might be substituted for the other without changing the meaning of the discussion. The partial identification of the terms with each other, and the occasional ease of substitution of one for the other, bespeaks a lack of discreteness in these basic concepts.

This confusion is due primarily to the fact that their connotations or definitions do not demarcate them but tend to identify them. This is especially true with reference to the important item of "meaning." The formal definition of the value designates that it has a "meaning" in addition to its "empirical content." Yet it seems that the "meaning" is also in the attitude.

. . . the effect of a social phenomenon depends in addition [to the empirical content] on the *subjective* (my italics) standpoint taken by the individual or the group toward this phenomenon, and can be calculated only if we know not only the objective content of the assumed cause, but also the meaning which it has at the given moment for the given conscious beings.[36]

These remarks suggest that the meaning is identified with the subjective standpoint. The tendency to assimilate the meaning into both the attitude and the value makes it difficult to regard them as separate entities, capable of a temporal and causal

[36] Vol. I, 38

relation to one another; instead, it suggests more that they are aspects of one another and exist in a single relation of unity. To hate a person is to view him as a hated object; as an object (or value), his "hated" character emerges with the attitude of hatred. They come into existence together as phases of one another. This suggests the logical difficulty of taking them as separate entities with changeable temporal and causal relations to one another.

In the light of these logical difficulties, it is not surprising that the methodological scheme of a law of social becoming proves to be fragile. This scheme declares that a value playing upon a pre-existing attitude gives rise to a new attitude, or an attitude playing upon a pre-existing value gives rise to a new value. With terms that are uncertain and not clearly disjunctive, the presumed causal relation becomes suspect.

The questionable character of the scheme is increased by the problem as to how a value operates on an attitude, or an attitude on a value. This problem is either ignored or not admitted by the methodological principle itself, for the principle implies that an attitude and a value give rise in a deterministic way to a new attitude or value. Yet in the discussion which the authors have devoted to what they term "the definition of the situation," they do deal with the question as to how values act on attitudes, and they admit that instead of a predetermined outcome, multiple possibilities are present.

The definition of a situation refers to the way in which the individual interprets it so that he can act. A situation which is not defined is in an unformulated state; in defining it, different possibilities of behavior are present.

... the definition of the situation is a necessary preliminary to any act of will, for in given conditions and with a given set of attitudes an indefinite plurality of actions is possible . . . usually there is a process

[37] Vol. I, 68-69

of reflection after which either a ready social definition is applied or a new personal definition worked out.[37]

This suggests that the formation of a new attitude in such a situation does not occur in the set fashion that the methodological formula assumes. The effect of the value is mediated by a process of reflection, implying the possibility of a variety of reactions.

These points which have been made with reference to the methodological formula[38] throw it into distinct question as a workable scheme for social research. Indeed, as we have already mentioned, it is practically ignored in the actual study of the Polish peasant society. This, in itself, suggests some realization of its unsuitability.

Yet, while this formula is essentially ignored, great use is made of the methodological scheme in its broader outlines, i.e., the objective factor of culture and social organization and the subjective factor of personal experience and orientation. In the analysis of their materials, the authors are dealing with these factors and are seeking to trace their interactions, so that, while there is virtually no attempt to isolate laws of social becoming, the methodological scheme in its general character is used in the handling and in the interpretation of the materials on the Polish peasant.

This last point should be made clear. As we have mentioned previously, the methodological approach proposed by Thomas and Znaniecki can and must be viewed on two levels. The first level merely represents the general realization that in social life the influence of cultural and objective factors is dependent on the disposition of individuals and that, consequently, this subjective factor enters into the social life as a vital aspect that

[38] By "methodological formula," I refer to the authors' declaration that a combination of a specific attitude and a specific value leads to a new specific attitude or value, and hence that the isolation of this relation would yield a law.

[27]

cannot be ignored. The second level of the conception takes the form of presupposing that the relation between the objective and the subjective factors is of the definite sort that is asserted by the methodological formula. Even though the second conception may be invalid, the first may be valid. Indeed, this seems to be the case. On logical grounds, the methodological formula as a device for securing laws of social becoming is fallacious; the fact that it is not seriously employed by the authors is further evidence of this. However, the general view seems distinctly valid; it is consistently adhered to by the authors in the development of their theoretical schemes and in their analysis and interpretation of Polish peasant life. As the discussion has already indicated, it is a view which recognizes the role of human experience in social life. It realizes that the study of social life needs first to ascertain the orientation or attitudes of individuals on whom social influences are acting, and second, to follow the experience of such individuals as they act in reference to such influences.

To use this view effectively in research and study, it is necessary to secure data on this subjective factor. Such data must meet scientific requirements: they must be empirical; and they must have the permanency that always makes them accessible to other students. Thomas and Znaniecki have proposed the "human document" as the means of securing these subjective data and preserving them in "objective" form. This proposal is a major contribution and has exercised a great influence on contemporary sociology. We are now ready to turn to its consideration.

THE USE OF HUMAN DOCUMENTS

The materials which Thomas and Znaniecki have used almost exclusively in their study of Polish peasant society are in the form of human documents. The human document is an account of individual experience which reveals the individual's actions as a human agent and as a participant in social life. Such documents are given in great quantity in the volumes and presumably contain the source data for the analyses and interpretations made by the authors.

Subsequently, after we review the treatment which the authors make of the various materials, we shall have occasion to consider critically the significance of human documents for social research. The only comment that needs to be made here is that they are well adapted, logically, to the study of the "subjective aspect" of culture.

The materials, or human documents, are primarily of five kinds: letters; life histories (particularly autobiographies); intimate newspaper accounts; court records; and records of social agencies. The consideration of these will be in the order of mention.

1. *Use of letters.* The greater part of the first volume (of the two volume edition) consists of a large number of letters, representing the correspondence between members of given family groups: between husbands and wives; and between persons outside of family and marriage relations. Exactly fifty series of such letters are given; each series is grouped under a family name; there are 764 separate letters. The letters are primarily either to or from emigrants. The series represent different sectors of peasant life; that is, the letters have been collected from peasant groups living in different portions of what is now Poland, and representing different levels of Polish society such as the peasant nobility, the manor peasants, the peasant proletariat, and the peasants who have become resident in towns and industrial communities.

The authors tell us that these letters are the "concrete materials" upon which their characterization and analysis of Polish peasant life are based.[39] This characterization and this analysis have been arrived at inductively from the letters.

The analysis of the attitudes and characters given in the notes to particular letters and in introductions to particular series contains nothing not essentially contained in the materials themselves . . . the synthesis constituting the introductions to particular volumes is also based upon the materials. . . .[40]

It is important to remember this point in view of the extensive scope of the characterization and interpretation which the authors have given. What they refer to as the "introduction to particular volumes" is a lengthy preface of 215 pages devoted to a characterization of Polish peasant society. In addition, each series of letters has a theoretical introduction. Finally, an enormous number of footnotes are given to the letters, representing theoretical comments on the letters.

It is not necessary to give any extensive reproduction of the lengthy preface in which the authors analyze and interpret Polish peasant life; but a brief résumé is needed in order to see how they have used the letters as material. In their elaborate statement, they present a theoretical description of Polish peasant society in its main phases: the peasant family; marriage; the class system; social environment; economic life; religious and magical attitudes; and the theoretic and aesthetic interests of the peasant. These phases of life are discussed from the point of view of *change* and *transition* precipitated by social, economic, and political forces, by the industrialization of cities and towns, and by the proletarization of the peasant. The important element in this general introduction is the implication made by the authors regarding a scheme of economic evolution which affected the peasant society. The thesis is a series of sequences and effects: an emancipation of peasants

[39] Vol. I, 76   [40] Vol. I, 76

from the social opinion dominant in their communities; a process of individualization; the disintegration of family life; the emergence of marriage groups as central units in place of previous larger families; the departure from tradition; and the emergence of a new concept of the family and of a new conception of personal relations.

The introductions to the separate series of letters and the theoretical notes to different letters deal in general with these same themes.

The authors declare that the elaborate characterization of Polish peasant society which they present is based on the material contained in the letters. The inductive procedure which they presumably have followed to arrive at the characterization is through the application of their methodological scheme. Referring to the use of the letters, they say:

> The general character of the work is mainly that of a systematization and classification of attitudes and values prevailing in a concrete group. Every attitude and every value ... can be really understood only in connection with the whole social life of which it is an element, and therefore this method is the only one that gives us a full and systematic acquaintance with all the complexity of social life.[41]

> ... its task [that of analysis] is only to isolate single attitudes, to show their analogies and dependencies, and to interpret them in relation to the social background upon which they appear.[42]

> In addition to the exhibition of various attitudes, these letters show the primitive familial organization in its relation to the problems which confront the group in the various situations of life. These situations are conditioned either by normal internal and external processes and events to which the familial organization was originally adapted—birth, growth, marriage, death of members of the group, normal economic conditions, traditional social environment, traditional religious life—or by new tendencies and new external influences to which the familial organization was not originally adapted, such as the increase of instruction and the dissemination of new ideas, economic and social advance, change of occupation, change of social environment through emigration to cities, to America, and to Germany, and contact with neighboring nationalities, mainly the Russian and German.[43]

[41] Vol. I, 77   [42] Vol. 1, 76   [43] Vol. I, 316

[31]

In the treatment of the letters, then, Thomas and Znaniecki apply their methodological approach to a body of materials and, on the basis of the attitudes and values which are determined, they characterize a complex society undergoing extensive social changes.

The purpose of our analysis is not to judge the correctness of the characterization of Polish peasant society given by the authors. Indeed, the materials would not permit the reader to do so—a point which we will consider later. It is sufficient to state here that the characterization is convincing and illuminating, and gives the impression of deep insight and of a high order of intelligence. Our interest is to consider the use made of the letters and to judge them as a methodological device in the light of what the authors claim for them.

A careful study of the letters does not bear out the major claims of the authors in this respect, since it is clear that the letters get their meaning and significance from the introductions and footnotes rather than vice versa. Were an intelligent reader with no knowledge of Polish culture or peasant life given merely the letters to study, it is inconceivable, in the judgment of the writer, that he could ever arrive at the characterization of Polish peasant society presented by the authors. For the reader to derive from these letters the generalizations, interpretations, and characterizations which they are supposed to yield, it is necessary for him to familiarize himself with these theoretical characterizations as they are given in the introductions to the different series and in the running comments in the footnotes. Without such theoretical guides, the reader, however careful, diligent, intelligent, and sensitive to human experience, would certainly miss a great deal of the analytic and interpretative meaning which Thomas and Znaniecki give to the different series of letters. And the extra step, that of constructing out of the letters the elaborate and systematic depiction of Polish peasant life as it is given in the general introduction, is inconceivable.

Careful and reflective study of the letters, as well as the general plan of treatment of the authors, compels one to recognize that it is the general introduction which is the framework for the separate introductions and for the theoretical notes, and that all three together are necessary to aid in the intelligent understanding of the letters. Indeed, some recognition is given to this point by the authors. Referring to the analyses as given in the notes to particular letters, they say:

Our acquaintance with the Polish society simply helps us in noting data and relations which would perhaps not be noticed so easily by one not immediately acquainted with the life of the groups.[44]

The extensiveness of this aid is much greater than is suggested by this modest note. The student might be confronted by these series of letters and yet would remain unaware of the most significant phenomena of the peasant society, if he were not to consult the elaborate notes by the authors and the introductions to the series of letters.

It seems quite clear that, in interpreting the letters, the authors have brought to bear upon them a framework of knowledge, information, and perspective that far transcends the letters themselves. This framework must have been based on an intimate knowledge of Polish peasant life, derived from a wide variety of sources; and on a rich fund of questions, hunches, leads, and ideas which sensitized the authors to special kinds of data and relations. They have given expression to this framework in their general introduction, and then used this scheme for the ordering and interpretation of the letters.

One may contend, perhaps, that the interpretation of the letters in this way is no violation of an inductive approach, in the sense that the letters become the test of the validity of the

[44] Vol. I, 76

[33]

schemes of interpretation. On this point, it may be said that often the interpretation of the authors seems quite strained; the reading of the letters before perusal of the introduction or notes makes one realize that the interpretative remarks exert a constraining influence on the reader. The crucial question here is whether the authors can supply methodological devices which would compel the impartial reader to agree that the letters bear out the interpretation. The authors are committed to such devices.

> We have to limit ourselves to certain theoretically important data, but we must know how to distinguish the data which are important. And every further step of the investigation will bring with it new methodological problems—analysis of the complete concrete data into elements, systematization of these elements, definition of social facts, establishing of social laws. All these stages of scientific procedure must be exactly and carefully defined if social theory is to become a science conscious of its own methods and able to apply them with precision . . .[45]

Despite this assertion, nowhere in their extensive discussions do the authors ever indicate how one can recognize an attitude or a value, or how one can "determine" that the attitude or the value is what the authors declare it to be. The validity of the designation can be tested only by the reader's judgment, and, frequently, the judgment is shaped by the interpretation given by the authors.

These considerations challenge the claim that the characterization of the Polish peasant society in all its complexity has been constructed out of the letter materials, and suggest a relation between the letters and the interpretation which neither has been recognized nor explained.

It should be remembered that the letters are being used, according to the authors' claim, as material from which knowledge of the whole complex society can be constructed. This involves the necessity of considering things in their context,

[45] Vol. I, 19-20

a point which the authors are at pains to emphasize. With reference to the analysis of the letters, they declare, "Every attitude and every value can be really understood only in connection with the whole social life of which it is an element . . ."[46] In this respect the letters do not meet the methodological requirements. Taken individually, each family series does not depict the continuity of life or the complete social personalities within the context of a whole social group. Instead, the letters are fragmentary in character, revealing a local issue, a passing preoccupation, a glimpse of the complexity of situations involving family life, and, particularly, stressing interests, such as that of money, which are likely to be pronounced in relation to a member of the family who has emigrated to America. Having this fragmentary, incomplete, and discontinuous character, the letters are not suited to give a view of the "whole social life" which would guarantee against a distorted interpretation of the elements of attitudes and values.

Our judgment must be, then, that the letters are not suited for the kind of interpretative use which is contained in the claims advanced by the authors. They are not extensive enough or well rounded enough to cover all phases of the whole social life; nor are they sufficiently continuous to cover the period of change. Their significance seems to depend on an approach within a well-rounded theoretical framework; a framework which is not formed by a study of the letters themselves. As suggested, this sets the problem anew as to what is the possible use and value of these letters as human documents.

The problem is an important one. That the letters have use, value, and significance must be apparent to any impartial reader even though he be thoroughly disillusioned over the validity of the special claims advanced by the authors. If one

[46] Vol. I, 77

reads carefully and reflectively the mass of letters, he does form vivid impressions of certain interests of the peasants: such as a love for land, an interest in work, sentiments of family solidarity, attitudes toward nature, religious inclinations, and so forth. He may also form some appreciation of disintegrative processes such as the breaking of traditional attitudes, the development of economic ambitions and "climbing tendencies," the dissolution of family solidarity, and the breakdown of family and community control. Therefore, while the letter materials do not bear out the methodological claims, it would be absurd to waive them aside as of no value.

At this point, one is presented with a problem that is very important in social research: the problem of the value of documentary materials which do not meet the rigid application of scientific canons. If one applies to each letter or series of letters which Thomas and Znaniecki present, the test considerations usually employed in evaluation of source data, it is clear that shortcomings exist. These test considerations include representativeness of the data; adequacy of the data; reliability of the data; and validity of the interpretation of the data. With reference to representativeness, we are not told how the authors collected their letters nor how they made their selections. On the matter of adequacy, we are told virtually nothing concerning the life, setting, and background of the families or individuals; further, the content of the letters seems fragmentary, dealing with occasional and selected experiences and not covering the totality of interests of the writers. In the case of reliability of experiences cited, we are given no means of testing the honesty or truthfulness of the account. Finally, with reference to interpretation, there is no way of understanding how the interpretation was arrived at; nor are there any rules which would permit determination as to whether the interpretation is correct or erroneous, or the extent to which it is so.

The failure of the separate letters to measure up in these respects would rather largely condemn them as source material for scientific research. Yet, again, to set them aside as having no scientific value or use would be to show a different set of shortcomings and to ignore the understanding, insight, and appreciation which their careful reading yields. These considerations set the problem of the value and use of the letters as source material.

This problem, which transcends the present work by Thomas and Znaniecki, can be best considered with reference to their work. First, it should be pointed out that while the letters taken separately fall down before the application of the criteria of which we have spoken, taken collectively they fare much better. There is a large measure of verification and support which the letters give one another; pieced together, they tend to give consistent pictures. Since the letters are numerous, since they were not written with thought of their subsequent scientific use, and since the different series were collected independently of one another, the fact that they do fit together and support one another must be taken seriously. Thus, while one might throw out each letter on the ground of test criteria, and thus throw out all of them, their collective consideration would compel one to recognize in them a representativeness, a certain adequacy, and a reliability that cannot be ignored. The point represented in these remarks should be given consideration in present controversial discussions concerning the scientific value of human documents.

The problem should be considered further, with reference to the value of the letters for interpretative purposes. It is clear, as we have stated above, that the letters presented by Thomas and Znaniecki are not the inductive materials out of which they have constructed their elaborate analysis of Polish peasant life. It is equally clear, however, that the letters are not mere illustrative material for the exemplification of their theoretical analyses. The actual relation is somewhere in between. The numerous and thoughtful notes to the letters give us every reason to believe that the authors mulled over the letters a great deal and derived much from them in the way of ideas, suggestions, and generalizations which they incorporated into their theoretical statements. There is equal reason to believe that they already had a rather extensive theoretical scheme (built out of experience that had nothing to do with the letters) with which they approached the letters and which guided and frequently coerced their interpretation of the letters. Thus, there has been an interaction between theory and inductive material, but an interaction which is exceedingly ambiguous.

With respect to the more pointed question as to how satisfactory the letters are for testing the theoretical statements of the authors, one has to give an indecisive reply. Frequently, they are very satisfactory, for at times the content of the letters clearly bears out the interpretation and at other times shows the interpretation to be quite forced. Usually, however, one cannot decide definitely; the interpretation merely seems to be plausible. With respect to these instances where the letters are unsatisfactory as a test of the theoretical interpretation, two things may be said. First, one must admit, as the authors would, that the letters are far from being as satisfactory as one would wish them to be. This accounts for some of the inadequacy of the letters as inductive tests. But the other point must be mentioned also. It is the paradoxical point that even though the letter be as perfect as is conceivably possible, and even though it seems to bear out the interpretation, it need not be the requisite test. Especially, in the case of more embracing conceptions, the theory may have to be tested by other things than the letters to which it is being applied. This seems to be true in the case of several of the authors' theoretical views.

Generally, with respect to the authors' use of letters as human documents, it may be said that the letters considered by themselves are not very meaningful; it is also clear that the theoretical analyses, if left to stand by themselves, would be formal, abstract, and rather dogmatic. The merging of the two does yield a concreteness and appreciative understanding that cannot be stated either as a mere illustration of the theory, nor as an inductive grounding of that theory. There seems to be involved a new relation, perhaps more in the nature of a psychological than of a logical relation, that so far has not been stated or made clear.

2. *Life Histories as Human Documents.* Thomas and Znaniecki employ the "life history" as another kind of material that will provide data for social theory. Indeed, they regard it as "the most perfect type of sociological material." We quote their formal statement:

Whether we draw our materials for sociological analysis from detailed life records of concrete individuals or from the observation of mass-phenomena, the problems of sociological analysis are the same. But even when we are searching for abstract laws life-records of concrete personalities have a marked superiority over any other kind of materials. We are safe in saying that personal life-records, as complete as possible, constitute the *perfect* type of sociological material, and that if social science has to use other materials at all it is only because of the practical difficulty of obtaining at the moment a sufficient number of such records to cover the totality of sociological problems, and of the enormous amount of work demanded for adequate analysis of all personal materials necessary to characterize the life of a social group. If we are forced to use mass-phenomena as material, or any kind of happenings taken without regard to the life-histories of the individuals who participate in them, it is a defect, not an advantage of our present sociological method.[47]
... The more complete a sociological document becomes the more it approaches a full personal life record.[48]

[47] Vol. II, 1832-33   [48] Vol. II, 1833-34

There are a number of ways in which the personal life record has special usefulness. First, it is regarded as being superior for the simple task of characterizing attitudes and values.

Indeed it is clear that even for the characterization of single social data—attitudes and values—personal life records give us the most exact approach. An attitude as manifested in an isolated act is always subject to misinterpretation, but this danger diminishes in the very measure of our ability to connect this act with past acts of the same individual.[49]

By virtue of enabling a more precise determination of attitudes and values, the life record is also best suited to the nomothetic purpose of ascertaining abstract social laws. The authors believe that it provides the material suitable to the isolation of laws of social becoming in accordance with their methodological formula.

A third way in which the life history may be of special value is in enabling one to trace the career of an attitude and follow its evolution thru a series of experiences. Since the life history presents the person in the process of evolution, it permits one to see the emergence of an attitude as a result of a line of development. The authors refer to this as a "line of genesis."

The application of sociological generalization to social personalities requires thus, first of all, the admission of what we may call *typical lines of genesis*. A line of genesis is a series of facts through which a certain attitude is developed from some other attitude (or group of attitudes), a value from some other value (or group of values), when it does not develop directly, and the process cannot be treated as a single elementary fact. For example there is probably no social influence that could produce directly an attitude of appreciation of science from the parvenu's pride in his wealth, no intellectual attitude that could directly lead an untrained individual to produce a scientifically valid concept from the data of common-sense observation; but by a series of intermediary stages the parvenu can become a sincere protector of science, by a more or less long training in theoretic research a student learns to produce scientific values. In such a series every single link is a fact of the type:

[49] Vol. II, 1833

[40]

attitude—value—attitude, or: value—attitude—value, and as such, if properly analyzed, can always be explained by sociological law (or lead to the discovery of a sociological law), but the series as a whole cannot be subject to any law, for there are many possible ways in which an attitude can be developed out of another attitude, a value out of another value.[50]

Finally, the life history is of particular value in that it enables one to follow the whole process of personal evolution, and, so to ascertain the nature of social personality, and to characterize it as a type. This point will require some explanation, particularly since it is of primary importance in the authors' views. The authors believe that the theory of social personality[51] requires the student to "reconstruct the entire process of every personal evolution from single facts." The personality is something that exists in the form of evolution; it develops, matures, and changes. Consequently, it shows itself only in "the course of its total life."

> The essential points, which cannot be here sufficiently emphasized, are that the social personality as a whole manifests itself only in the course of its total life and not at any particular moment of its life, and that its life . . . is a continuous evolution in which nothing remains unchanged. This evolution often tends toward a stabilization as its ultimate limit, but never attains this limit completely; and even then it is not this limit as such, but the very course of evolution tending to this limit, that constitutes the main object matter of socio-psychological synthesis.[52]

Personality is viewed, then, as a personal organization in evolution, and one has to characterize it in this developmental aspect. It is not static and so it can not be ascertained from a "cross-sectioning" of the individual in some period in his life. Instead, to determine its nature, one has to follow the progressive formation of the individual. This becomes a problem of synthesis of the attitudes and values of the person. Now the life history is a record which permits one to follow the

[50] Vol. II, 1839
[51] We shall present and discuss this theory later.
[52] Vol. II, 1837-38

[41]

developing career of the person; as such it is of special value as material for social theory.

Correlative with the need of determining the nature of social personality, is that of establishing *types* of personality, i.e., the different classes of personality.

... the concept of type plays the same part in social synthesis as the concept of causal fact plays in social analysis, the aim of the former being to find classes, just as the latter is to find laws.[53]

The life record in permitting one to ascertain the personality also serves as the device for determining personality types.

These four ways (isolation of attitudes and values, isolation of laws of social becoming, isolation of lines of genesis, and determination of personality) in which the life history may be used are the primary reasons why the authors regard it as a superior kind of material for social theory. It should be realized that these ways of using the life history fit in with the fundamental view of the authors that social life may be viewed as an interaction between objective organization and subjective experience.

Thomas and Znaniecki present in their work a lengthy life record which occupies 312 pages of fine print. It is an autobiography written (at the request of the authors) by a Polish emigrant who is named Władek. Thomas and Znaniecki devote a few introductory remarks to the autobiography. They have made copious comments, in the form of notes, throughout the autobiography. Finally, they give a conclusion of some 18 pages in which they characterize in general and abstract terms the personality of Władek and trace its formation in different social settings. The autobiography and their remarks concerning it represent "an attempt to reconstruct a personal life-record from the standpoint outlined above (i.e., the uses to which the life record can be put) and by the methods of

[53] Vol. II, 1837

social psychology as determined in the methodological note prefacing Vol. I of this work." We are given the means, then, of making some test of the claims which the authors advance in favor of the personal life record.

The second and third of the claims as we have mentioned them, may be dismissed immediately. In their study of the extensive autobiography of Władek, the authors have not been able to produce or establish any laws of social becoming. They have suggested a few instances in which a designated attitude is a product of a designated value playing upon a pre-existing attitude; but these suggestions are hypothetical and are not established by the material in the account, and so few are even these faltering instances that we can say that they have not been able to bear out this claim in the case of the life record of Władek. Their experience has been similar with reference to the determination of "lines of genesis." Despite the extensiveness of the document, with its minuteness of detail as to experience, and although the authors say much to the effect that lines of genesis are present in Władek's career, they do not isolate and establish such a sequence of attitude development. The verification of this claim, then, has not been made in their treatment of Władek's autobiography.

What we have said regarding the letter materials applies in the case of the life record as far as the first claim is concerned: the use of such a document to "determine single attitudes and values." In their numerous notes, the authors refer to experiences of Władek as indicating such and such an attitude or such and such a value. Since we have no methodological rule which enables us to determine a given attitude, we are forced to use our judgment as to whether the given experience is an instance of the attitude or value that the authors claim it to be. Relying merely on one's judgment, one must say that frequently the experience does seem to represent the attitude that the authors propose; in other instances, that the designation is likely; in others, that it is uncertain; and in still others, that it is forced. It is true that the fuller context provided by the life record increases the assurance of one's judgment in comparison to the interpretation of letters; otherwise, the question concerning the designation of attitudes in the letters applies to this task in the case of the autobiography.

Essentially the same remarks can be made with reference to the use of the autobiography to determine the personality of Władek and to trace its evolution. This touches intimately on the whole question of interpretation which we will take up shortly. It is sufficient to indicate here that the authors have striven to use the life record to show the nature and evolution of a type of personality, but that their effort must face the same sort of question raised in connection with the letters.

The criteria that we have spoken of in the case of the letter materials (representativeness, adequacy, reliability, and validity of interpretation) can be applied to the life record of Władek. Following the same order, one may ask, first, how representative is the life record? We are told by Thomas and Znaniecki that "he is a typical representative of the culturally passive mass which . . . constitutes in every civilized society the enormous majority of the population." There is no demonstrable proof of this assertion; indeed, it is hard to see how it can be proven. The theoretical treatment which they give to the life record gives plausibility to their view, but this is so only in the event that one accepts the theoretical scheme with which they approach the life record.

Even such an extensive and voluminous account as Władek's is open to question on the ground of adequacy. The fact that there is difficulty so frequently in characterizing attitudes, and especially in determining positively the evolution of Władek's personality, testifies to this shortcoming. If this is true in the case of the authors, it must be recognized to be much truer in the case of the reader.

It is with reference to the third criterion, reliability of the account, that questions become especially acute. Nowadays these questions are conventional, and they apply to Władek's autobiography. Is the account truthful? Is it sincere? Did Władek write it with a certain kind of audience in mind? Did he "dress it up"? Is his memory reliable? Such, and other similar questions can be raised. There is little in the account itself which permits us to answer these questions. The authors declare that the "sincerity of the autobiography is unmistakable," and that the comparison with letters from his family disclose no voluntary omissions. (These letters are not given in the work.) They explain what they regard to be the sources of inexactness in the account, and being aware of them, are prepared against fallacious interpretation. On these various points, the authors may be correct; the reader, however, has no way of being sure. Indeed, the account itself easily suggests a different character. Władek seems keenly bent on telling a story, is appreciative of dramatic depiction, and, consequently, is consistently providing intriguing endings. The account is filled with surprise elements and bespeaks clever handling. There is little doubt that in Władek we are dealing with a highly imaginative mind with a flair for story telling that welcomed the chance of giving vent to the latent inclination to write. Whether this impression is true is not important. We wish merely to stress that one may raise genuine doubts concerning the reliability of the account without being able to have such doubts dispelled by the account or by what the authors say about it.

With respect to the last point, the validity of the authors' interpretation, we wish chiefly to emphasize that the authors approach this task with a fairly elaborate theory of personality. We will explain this theory later. They seek to interpret Władek's life record from the standpoint of this theory. In doing so, they give some evidence of ordering the experiences so as to fit inside the theoretical framework. Frequently, one has strong suspicions of the imposition of a theory on the experiences; in such instances, while the interpretation (which is practically always plausible) may be true, the recorded experiences do not enable one to determine whether it is true. One instance may be given to illustrate the point. Referring to his childhood, Władek says:

> I always considered disobedience a sin and I could not understand how it was possible not to listen to one's parents. I listened not only to them but also to my older brothers and sisters, and if they ordered me to do anything I did it, not only from fear but also from conviction that I was doing right. Neither my parents nor my older brothers and sisters ever complained of me in this respect.[54]

The interpretation which the authors make of this in a footnote is as follows:

> The obedience here is the result of the desire for response, but Władek claims moral merit on this account, as he always does when his behavior happens to be in accord with the social norm, even when its source is quite other than the feeling of duty—a typical Philistine attitude. His claim is also a proof that in the process of dissolution of the old familial solidarity obedience is the most persistent of all the attitudes. The bond of affection which substitutes itself in other cases for the primitive solidarity is a socially new attitude, not belonging, like obedience, to the traditional complex.[55]

These things the authors say may be true, but the account itself does not permit one to judge. It may be pointed out that the interpretation given by the authors fits in nicely with their general theoretical scheme.

On this problem of interpretation, we are confronted with

[54] Vol. II, 1943   [55] Vol. II, 1943

the same situation that has been mentioned in the case of the letter materials. It is very clear that Władek's autobiography (or others which the authors may have had) is not the inductive material from which they have constructed their theory of personality. It is also clear that it is not a record which merely enables them to illustrate their theory. The primary question is whether it enables one to test, inductively, their theory. To this, a categorical reply cannot be given. For, while the experiences given frequently have a tough, independent character which enables them to be a test of a theoretical conception, at other times they seem, metaphorically speaking, to be helpless before the imposition of a theoretical view. To this problem we shall return later.

3. *Other Forms of Human Documents*. The remaining type of documents which Thomas and Znaniecki employ in their works are primarily the following: (1) Polish newspaper accounts chiefly in the form of reportorial letters from local correspondents; (2) records of Polish church parishes in this country, and of Polish-American societies; (3) records of social agencies; and (4) court records. The newspaper accounts are used as the materials in the discussion of the disorganization and reorganization of peasant society in Poland. The church records and society records are presented in connection with the characterization of the nature and development of Polish-American communities and of Polish-American societies. The other two types of materials, records of social agencies and court records, are employed in the discussion of the disorganization of the Polish immigrant in this country.

For our purpose, it is not necessary to treat separately these different forms of documents and materials. These documents are quite different in general character from letters and life records. They are more formal and reflective, less intimate, personal, and naïve. We quote the remarks of the authors:

The materials which we are using in this volume have naturally a much less direct and personal character than those used in the first volume. Most of them come from popular newspapers and institutions; some have been collected by ourselves in personal investigation; some are systematically presented by other writers. Almost every document, even a peasant letter written to a newspaper, was consciously made by its author to bear on some particular question, is a product of a more or less methodical reflection about social phenomena; none is as naïve and unreflective as, for instance, a family letter. While this character of the documents makes their understanding relatively easy for the reader, it forces us to rely much less than in the earlier volumes on the intrinsic value of each document in particular and much more on their selection and systematic organization.[56]

With reference to their division dealing with the Polish immigrant, they say:

In the first part of the study, where our task is to describe synthetically and to explain genetically the general structure of Polish-American society, we shall have to leave out most of the materials on which our conclusions are based and use documents rather as examples helping the reader to understand certain particular aspects of the situation than as proofs of the truth of our statements, which can be sufficiently verified by going to the sources quoted. On the contrary, in the second part where our problem is to analyze typical cases of individual disorganization, we shall give, as far as possible within the limits of this volume, the concrete data from which our generalizations are drawn.[57]

Because of their more formal and less personal nature, the materials in the form of newspaper accounts, records of agencies, court records, parish records, etc., are not as revealing as letters and life records. Consequently, the reader will discover that their meaning depends even more than the letters and the life record on the body of interpretative theory which the authors bring to bear upon them. In general, they are fragmentary as human documents. In interpreting them, the authors are led to give them some meaning which the reading of the separate document, independent of the authors' remarks, frequently does not reveal. In this instance, while the interpretation is plausible, it is not attested by the document

[56] Vol. II, 1122-23   [57] Vol. II, 1478-79

itself, even though approached with the aid of the authors' theoretical scheme. What I have in mind is shown by the following case which is not singular or unrepresentative of the general use made of these documents by the authors. The account is in the form of a correspondent's letter to a popular Polish newspaper.

Josef Pawlowski, blacksmith from the village of Parchocin, after bidding good-bye to his young wife and two little children, had to go, as soldier of the reserve, to the distant war in Manchuria. The woman was pretty and, what is worse, fickle. Temptations came; she could not resist and went the wrong way. Having colluded with her lover, a young boy, she sold whatever she could—cows, pigs, grain from the barn—obtained a passport for (a journey) abroad and, taking the money and the bed-furnishings, ran away at night from her children sleeping in a cradle. She covered them with straw and left them so without pity. It seems that she went to America. . . . The husband did not perish in war; six weeks ago he even sent 50 roubles home.[58]

The interpretation made of this case by Thomas and Znaniecki is as follows:

Sexual love alone is not back of the woman's behavior. We must assume a strong desire for new experience which not only induced her to leave home and children but probably prepared the way for her new love. It is desire for new experience, stirred up by the possibilities which the break of the community isolation offers, that accounts for at least 50 per cent of the emigration to America and of season-emigration to Germany—desire for economic advance being the other important factor. And, while a young girl or a man has many ways in which his desires for new experience can be satisfied, a married peasant woman with children is practically forced to resign all aspirations in this line unless the whole family emigrates.[59]

Now there is no reason to believe that this interpretation is not true; on the other hand we do not know whether it is true. The fragmentary character of the record plus the fact that it is in the form of an observation made by an outsider makes it impossible to declare that the interpretation made in the first two sentences is true. The last two sentences of

[58] Vol. II, 1162   [59] Vol. II, 1162-63

[49]

the authors' interpretation are added in gratuitous fashion, and, of course, have no basis in the case at all. Nevertheless, the interpretation is not only plausible but is genuinely revealing, particularly in the light of the whole context of theoretical discussion and body of materials which the authors present in this division of their work; one has the feeling in the case of this single document, as in the instance of others, that even if the authors' interpretation were not true in the particular case, it would be generally true, and would be true in other particular cases.

From this particular instance, as well as from the treatment of the other documents, we have to infer the general procedure of the authors. It seems clear that they approach each document, and ask the question, "What does this document mean?" To the answering of the question, they bring, so to speak, a rich "apperception mass" based on an extensive and intimate acquaintance with Polish peasant life and also an appreciation and understanding of "human nature" which is organized under the influence of a series of theoretical schemes. Their interpretation is grounded partly in the document, partly in their broad theoretical background.

Here, again, we have to point out, as we have done above, that these documents (newspaper materials, organization records, court records, records of social agencies) cannot be regarded as the inductive basis of the authors' theoretical discussions, nor as mere illustrative materials for such theoretical views. This raises, again, the question as to the scientific value of human documents such as the authors have employed, and as to the mode of their use for scientific purposes. We wish to consider now this more general question, in the light of the authors' work.

4. *General Remarks on Human Documents.* A consideration should be made of the general reason why the authors

regard human documents of such importance. This regard follows logically from their basic notion of the subjective aspect of social life. The notion that individuals act toward objects in terms of the meaning which such objects have for them suggests the need of securing this subjective orientation in order to understand their activity. Whether one is interested in a specific instance of social or personal change, or in the general processes of personal evolution or social transformation, it is necessary to know the subjective factor which is involved. Study or research requires material which will reveal this subjective aspect.

Two quotations will indicate the basic conception on which the use of human documents rest.

> We must put ourselves in the position of the subject who tries to find his way in this world, and we must remember, first of all, that the environment by which he is influenced and to which he adapts himself, is *his* world, not the objective world of science—is nature and society as he sees them, not as the scientist sees them. The individual subject reacts only to his experience, and his experience is not everything that an absolutely objective observer might find in the portion of the world within the individual's reach, but only what the individual himself finds.[60]

> Since concrete social life is concrete only when taken together with the individual life which underlies social happenings, since the personal element is a constitutive factor of every social occurrence, social science cannot remain on the surface of social becoming, where certain schools wish to have it float, but must reach the actual human experiences and attitudes which constitute the full, live and active social reality beneath the formal organization of social institutions, or behind the statistically tabulated mass-phenomena which taken in themselves are nothing but symptoms of unknown causal processes and can serve only as provisional ground for sociological hypotheses.[61]

Human documents are the device by which one may "reach the actual human experiences and attitudes which constitute the full, live and active social reality." If one grants the validity of the contention that the "individual subject reacts only

[60] Vol. II, 1846-47   [61] Vol. II, 1834

[51]

to *his* (my italics) experience," one would need a device which would enable one to ascertain this experience. This is the function of the human document. The document may be thought of as preserving the experience; it is, in a sense, an objective record which the student may consult and to which he may return.

There is no question but what Thomas and Znaniecki have made a genuine contribution to sociological orientation in stressing the importance of the subjective factor, and in emphasizing the use of human documents as a source of materials on this factor.

One may ask, however, if the human documents which they employ in their work are suitable to the task of determining and characterizing the subjective factor; one may admit the theoretical value and need of human documents, and still raise the question as to how satisfactory are the *particular* documents which the authors have employed.

There can be little doubt about the shortcomings of these documents, as the above remarks on each kind of them have brought out. The application to them of the criteria of representativeness, adequacy, and trustworthiness do bring them into question. There are undoubtedly sociologists today who, on these very grounds, would reject essentially all of the documents in *The Polish Peasant* and, who, consequently, would regard the work as having no merit as an instance of scientific research.

Two points may be made with reference to this matter. In the first place, it should be realized that the authors are breaking ground, and are essentially pioneers in the form of investigation which they are advocating. Their basic aim, one should remember, is to exemplify "a standpoint and method," rather than to do a finished piece of social research. In handling their materials, they may be said to have realized this objective; they have shown the inescapable necessity of using human documents in *adequate*[62] social research, and they have illustrated the possibilities of such documents. There is reason to believe that the authors, themselves, are aware that their documentary material is not of the adequate or perfect character that would be essential for thoroughly reliable social research. The very fact that they speak of the "life record" as the *perfect* type of sociological material, yet employ in the main other kinds of documents, is in itself indicative of this. It may be said, on behalf of the authors, that they used the best documents *that they could secure;* it stands to reason that if better human documentary material had been accessible to them, they would have used it.[63]

No impartial reader can deny that the documentary materials given by Thomas and Znaniecki make understandable, to a large extent, their interpretations of Polish peasant life as well as the content of their social theory. As we have indicated, it is not merely as illustrative instances that the documentary material serves this purpose. While the documentary material readily lends itself to forced manipulation on behalf of some theoretical conception, and while Thomas and Znaniecki have yielded considerably to this temptation, nevertheless, much of the material has been approached by the authors in a genuine mood of impartial inquiry. In this respect, it has, therefore, a role other than a mere illustrative one. Much of it does serve as an inductive foundation for the theoretical interpretations of the authors. A further treatment of the role of human documents in social research will be given following a discussion of the authors' scheme of social theory.

---

[62] "Adequate" in the sense of having to include the factor of subjective human experience to understand human behavior, whether individual or collective.
[63] In this sense, their position is exactly like that of the historian or the ethnologist.

Part of the "standpoint and method" of Thomas and Znaniecki is their *social theory*. Some of the major outlines of this theory have already been given. It is based, as we have seen, on the major concepts of *attitude* and *value*. There is a special set of values of particular importance, namely, *social rules;* these rules form *institutions;* in their totality they constitute the *social organization* of a society.

Just as it is the province of sociology to study social values (in the form of rules), so it is the province of social psychology to study attitudes. The primary objective of both is to apply the methodological formula to attitudes and values in terms of their formation and so to arrive at laws of social becoming. We have already had occasion to consider this fundamental portion of their theory and to show its questionable possibility.

1. Theory of Personality. The other important objective of social psychology is to construct a theory of social personality. The authors' views on this task must now be given with some thoroughness. As we have seen, they view personality in terms of a scheme of personal development or an evolution of personal organization. This means that the task is that of synthesizing attitudes into "lines of genesis" and these into a pattern of personal evolution.

To develop a theory of personality that fits this dynamic view, the authors have been led to reduce personality to a number of constituent factors that could be handled in a developmental way. These fundamental constituents are temperament, character, and life organization. Temperament and character are defined by the authors as follows:

We may call temperament the fundamental original group of attitudes of the individual as existing independently of any social influences;

[54]

we may call character the set of organized and fixed groups of attitudes developed by social influences operating upon the temperamental basis.[64]

Temperamental attitudes may be regarded as original, native attitudes arising from impulse and corresponding to what the authors call "natural things." What is distinctly important about them is that they are not guided by any scheme or rule. Thus, the spontaneous hunger of an infant is such an attitude; food is the "natural thing." When such hunger comes under the conscious influence and control of a rule, or when its expression becomes "defined" in the conscious experience of the individual, it passes over into a character attitude. A character attitude, consequently, is one that is guided by a conscious scheme, and so, one which is intellectual and reflective.

This distinction indicates that the development of personality involves the organization of temperamental attitudes into a structure of character attitudes. This is done by means of rules, that is to say, the individual brings a temperamental attitude under the control of a reflective rule of understanding.

The totality of these rules by which the individual develops an organization of character attitudes constitutes the *life organization* of the individual. An idea of the nature of life organization is given by the following remarks of the authors. They declare that society does not want the individual

to react instinctively in the same way to the same material conditions, but to construct reflectively similar social situations, even if material conditions vary. The uniformity of behavior it tends to impose upon the individual is not a uniformity of organic habits but of consciously followed *rules*. The individual, in order to control social reality for his needs, must develop not series of uniform reactions, but general *schemes* of situations; his life-organization is a set of rules for definite

[64] Vol. II, 1844

situations, which may be even expressed in abstract formulas. Moral principles, legal prescription, economic forms, religious rites, social customs, etc., are examples of schemes.[65]

The character of the individual corresponds to his life organization; the rules and schemes of the individual determine and organize his character attitudes.

The process by which temperamental attitudes are formed into character attitudes under the influence of reflective schemes is of crucial importance to the views of the authors, and so must be entered into here in some detail. This process involves the interaction between the individual and his group.

In order to satisfy the social demands put upon his personality he must reflectively organize his temperamental attitudes; in order to obtain the satisfaction of his own demands, he must develop intellectual methods for the control of social reality in place of the instinctive ways which are sufficient to control natural reality.[66]

In the face of a social situation in which an individual has certain attitudes (in the form of wishes, motives, etc.), and in which he encounters demands made on his behavior, the individual has to organize his behavior. This is done by what the authors call "defining the situation." Sometimes the "definition" is already at hand in the form of a group prescription; sometimes, the individual is forced to evolve his own scheme of action. In either case, the individual has to form an interpretation of the situation, through a process of conscious reflection, involving a new organization of his behavior in that situation.

This process of "defining a situation" has two phases:

The first phase is characterized by an essential vagueness. The situation is quite undetermined; even if there are already in the individual wishes which will give significance to the new data, they are not sufficiently determined with regard to these data, and the complexity is not ordered,

[65] Vol. II, 1852-53   [66] Vol. II, 1851

values are not outlined, their relations are not established. In the second phase the situation becomes definite, the wish is crystallized and objectified, and the individual begins to control his new experience.[67]

In this process of defining a situation, the individual

...has to take social meanings into account, interpret his experience not exclusively in terms of his own needs and wishes, but also in terms of the traditions, customs, beliefs, aspirations of his social milieu.[68]

The points of importance in the process of defining a situation are: the need of making some reflective analysis of the situation, into which social values and the individual's needs enter as elements; the formation of a scheme which is the plan of meeting the situation and making it clear—the scheme becomes part of the individual's life organization; and the formation of an attitude in correspondence with this scheme —this attitude becomes part of character.

Two other points should be noted: first, that the situations are primarily social situations; and second, that temperament is incapable of defining such a situation. The following quotation presents these points:

In order to become a social personality in any domain the individual must therefore not only realize the existence of the social meanings which objects possess in this domain, but also learn how to adapt himself to the demands which society puts upon him from the standpoint of these meanings, and how to control these meanings for his personal purposes; and since meanings imply conscious thought, he must do this by conscious reflection, not by mere instinctive adaptation of reflexes.[69]

This quotation indicates that the definition of a situation involves an interaction between the group and the individual. The group exerts social demands; the individual strives to satisfy his needs inside of this situation.

Personal evolution is always a struggle between the individual and society—a struggle for self-expression on the part of the individual, for his subjection on the part of society—and it is in the total course of this

[67] Vol. II, 1847   [68] Vol. II, 1852   [69] Vol. II, 1850-51

struggle that the personality—not as a static 'essence' but as a dynamic, continually evolving set of activities—manifests and constructs itself.[70]

Thus, the authors declare that

The fundamental principles of personal evolution must be sought therefore both in the individual's own nature and in his social milieu.[71]

The process of personality formation inside of this struggle between individual expression and social conformity is guided by four fundamental tendencies—those basic traits which have come to be known as Thomas' four wishes. These are the wishes for new experience, security, response, and recognition. These wishes are manifested in the individual's attitudes and so are important in determining their formation.

New experience, which is based on curiosity, represents a break from established regularity. As such, it has two important aspects: one is that it is basic in defining a situation, "The factor making the individual perceive and define new situations is always his own, conscious or subconscious, desire for new experience";[72] the other aspect is that this desire represents a threat to the adherence to the rules of the group.

The wish for security is a tendency toward stability, and so, to the avoidance of certain experiences. It inclines the individual "to preserve the old form and range of activity in spite of the changed conditions and to be satisfied with the results that can be obtained in this way."[73] It becomes responsible for the preservation of a way of defining situations which the individual has formed.

Thomas and Znaniecki point out that the group seeks to suppress attitudes which are in disharmony with the existing social organization, or threaten to be, and to develop attitudes

[70] Vol. II, 1861-62
[71] Vol. II, 1859
[72] Vol. II, 1876
[73] Vol. II, 1878

and schemes required by existing social systems. The positive way by which this is accomplished is by capitalizing on the individual's desires for response and recognition. The desire for response—the desire "to obtain a direct positive personal response" from others—inclines the individual to adapt himself to the attitudes of others, and so it is generally "the strongest of all those attitudes by which harmony is maintained and dissension avoided between the members of a group." The desire for recognition is "probably the strongest factor pushing the individual to realize the highest demands which the group puts upon personal conduct."

As we shall point out later, the stabilization of attitudes on the basis of the devices for response and recognition becomes increasingly rare with the development of civilization and so increases the difficulties of social control. Society seeks to utilize them, however, to secure such control.

Just one further item needs to be mentioned to round out this abbreviated presentation of the authors' theory of personality, viz., their conception of personality type. They speak of three types—the Philistine, the Bohemian, and the creative individual. They are distinguished from each other from the standpoint of both character and life organization. In the Philistine, the set of attitudes constituting the character are so stable as practically to exclude the development of new attitudes. His life organization consists of a few narrow schemes which are sufficient to lead him through life, simply because he does not see problems which demand new schemes. The Bohemian is one whose character remains unformed and whose life organization consists of a number of inconsistent schemes. The creative individual is the type whose character may undergo systematic enlargement and whose life organization may expand according to some definite aims. These personality types represent divergent lines of development

[59]

inside of the struggle between individual expression and social control.

In this sketch of the theory of social personality as conceived by the authors, we see a scheme which embodies the interaction between the individual and the group; a scheme which is set in the framework of the subjective and objective aspects of social life. This latter conception, as we have seen, is the foundation to the entire work on the Polish peasant; the theory of personality in this sense, is an integral part of the entire structure of their views. Social life is recognized as an on-going process; personality is viewed from the standpoint of this movement of life. It is given a dynamic dimension, in the sense that the individual is engaged in a constant process of selecting from his milieu features which he must organize in order to act. Of these features, the demands and rules of his associates are of primary importance. The defining which he makes of them yields him a series of schemes and set of attitudes through which the temperament may ever threaten to break. These schemes and attitudes enter into the subsequent process of defining situations. In organizing his conduct in such a way as to reconcile the group's social demands and his own attitude-demands, the individual forms a characteristic mode of approach. This mode of approach serves as one basis for the determination of personality types.

It should be pointed out that this scheme of personality fulfills the intention which Thomas and Znaniecki announced of developing a type of social theory suited to a society undergoing change and reorganization. It is a view, then, adapted to the study of the changing character of Polish peasant society, in which the authors are interested.

As we have already mentioned, Thomas and Znaniecki apply their theory of personality to the life record of Władek, and so offer some means of giving it a test. The primary difficulty which is involved in this undertaking has already been pointed out, viz., the fact that at times their interpretations, in terms of the personality scheme, transcend the data and at other times order the data. Consequently, their analysis of Władek's experiences and personal make-up, while sometimes convincing and at other times plausible, cannot be said to yield the genuine test necessary to substantiate the validity of their scheme.

Perhaps the outstanding obstacle to an unqualified testing of their theory is that which plagues most of social science, i.e., the absence of definite guides or rules which would enable one to ascertain positively that a given datum is an instance of a given concept and so deserves its application. Thus, to illustrate, when Thomas and Znaniecki assert a given experience of Władek's to be a certain attitude or an expression of, let us say, a wish for response, or an indication of a Philistine personality, one has to rely on one's judgment as to the certainty of the application. Similarly, with respect to the more inclusive application of their whole theory, we are forced to rely here upon a judgment as to the reasonableness of their interpretation.

Perhaps all that can be said is that their theory of personality is very provocative, seems suited to the changing world in which we live, and has both a logical and empirical plausibility. It gives evidence of an extensive and intimate acquaintance with human beings in general and, in particular, with persons in a changing society; it indicates thoughtful preoccupation with problems of conduct revealed in the activities of such people; and it shows profound reasoning on such problems. It is not surprising that the views of Thomas and Znaniecki on the topic of personality should have exercised a profound influence on contemporary sociology and social psychology.

2. *Disorganization and Reorganization.* A major interest of Thomas and Znaniecki, as we have seen, has been to study a society that was undergoing change. The Polish peasant society is of this sort. In recent decades, it has been undergoing extensive change, showing considerable breaking down of the old order of life and the formation of a new order. Because of this character it was inevitable that a study such as that of the authors should be intimately concerned with problems of disorganization and reorganization. Indeed, it is just this aspect of Polish society which became central in their attention, leading them in their usual manner, to formulate a theory and to apply it to their data of Polish peasant life. In doing this, they have not only developed an interesting theoretical scheme of disorganization and reorganization (in both their individual and social aspects), but have also made a striking analysis of the ways in which these processes have operated in Polish peasant society.

We will present the essential outlines of their theory of disorganization and reorganization, considering these processes first on the social and then on the individual side. One prefatory remark may be made, namely, that it will be noted that their theory is based on the same fundamental idea of subjective attitude and objective value, and that, consequently, it is in conformity with other divisions of their theoretical structure.

3. *Theory of Social Disorganization and Reorganization.* Social disorganization is defined as a

decrease of the influence of existing social rules of behavior upon individual members of the group.[74]

The authors point out that "This decrease may represent innumerable degrees, ranging from a single break of some

[74] Vol. II, 1128

particular rule by one individual up to a general decay of all institutions of the group." Conceived in this broad way, social disorganization is to be found in some degree in all societies for "everywhere there are individual cases of breaking rules"; but in ordinary conditions of social stability such instances are controlled or prevented from spreading to others by reinforcing existing rules with the help of existing social sanctions. When instances of disorganization can no longer be checked by attempts to reinforce the existing rules, then social disorganization comes to be widely prevalent and leads to the dissolution of the group.

In the light of this conception, the problem becomes that of explaining why a social rule loses its efficacy and why it can no longer be reinforced. The answer is in terms of the general methodological principle which the authors have developed in their work. A given social rule (a value) is supported or maintained by a combination of attitudes; now, if new attitudes appear, the rule appears differently to those who have the new attitudes and its influence is correspondingly disturbed and lessened.

This means that the task of explaining social disorganization requires discovery of the nature of new attitudes which cause the rule to be differently valued, and discovery of the causes of these new attitudes. If the matter is put this way, as the authors remark, then there is no possibility of establishing "laws of social disorganization," for presumably the same attitudes may support a rule under one situation; under another, they may be new, and challenge that rule. One may, however, determine "laws of social becoming" in the instance of the new attitudes by tracing how they came into existence. In any particular instance of social disorganization, the problem would become one of determining new attitudes which disturbed the given rule or rules. The next step would be to ascertain the new values which caused the new attitudes.

An application of this scheme to the disorganization which the authors find among Polish peasant families and communities will help to make clearer the nature of the theory. The essential factors are the appearance of "individualistic" tendencies or attitudes among the peasants as a result of their contact with the outside world, particularly through seasonal emigration to Germany. These individualistic tendencies are primarily in the form of hedonistic interests (the desire for new kinds of pleasures) and new individual success tendencies. These individualistic tendencies (or attitudes) are formed in response to new values encountered in the outside world, such as alcoholic drinks, new foods, new forms of sex appeals, new vanity values, and individualistic types of economic organization. The new individualistic attitudes are in opposition to the "we"-attitudes on which the maintenance of the peasant family system depends. Now, traditionally, peasant society maintains its rules by its control of the individual's wish for response and his wish for recognition. The individual's desire for response leads him to seek acceptance and appreciation by the members of his family and community; his desire for recognition causes him to want the approbation of his community. These wishes lead him to preserve family solidarity and to adhere to community rules. When, however, his new individualistic attitudes become more important than his desires for the response or recognition of others, the rules of the group lose their efficiency; or if the social opinion of the group decays so that the group is not interested in using the individual's desires for response or recognition to cause him to conform to rules, such rules likewise become weak. In these events, a state of social disorganization becomes prevalent.

This is the theoretical way in which the authors explain the disorganization of Polish peasant society. This disorganization amounts to a breakdown of the rules which constituted the old primary group organization. This decay in influence of these rules is the result of the emergence of individualistic tendencies and the weakening of social opinion.[75] The new attitudes "cannot be adequately controlled by the old social organization because they cannot find an adequate expression in the old primary-group institutions."

The efforts to preserve the old rules are likely to be successful only in the event that outside contacts are limited. They become ineffective if the outside contacts increase and extend to all fields of life. For under such conditions, the entrance of new values into the experience of people on an extensive scale occasions an increasing number of new attitudes which in turn weaken the existing rule. This gives rise, the authors point out, to a different problem.

The problem is then no longer how to suppress the new attitudes, but how to find for them institutional expression, how to utilize them for socially productive purposes, instead of permitting them to remain in a status where they express themselves merely in individual revolt and social revolution.[76]

This sets the task for social reorganization. The general nature of social reorganization can be stated best in the words of the authors.

The decay of the traditional social organization is, as we have seen, due to the appearance and development of new attitudes leading to activities which do not comply with the socially recognized and sanctioned schemes of behavior. The problem of social reconstruction is to create new schemes of behavior—new rules of personal conduct and new in-

---

[75] It is of interest to note that the authors believe that the disintegration of social life organized on a primary group basis always follows from such individualistic tendencies and such weakening of primary group opinion. Accordingly, their theory would especially apply to contemporary civilized life which is marked by these very happenings.
[76] Vol. II, 1121

stitutions—which will supplant or modify the old schemes and correspond better to the changed attitudes, that is, which will permit the latter to express themselves in action and at the same time will regulate their active manifestations so as not only to prevent the social group from becoming disorganized but to increase its cohesion by opening new fields for social cooperation.[77]

The "task is to discover and understand the new attitudes which demand an outlet, to invent the schemes of behavior which would best correspond to these attitudes, and to make the group accept these schemes as social rules or institutions."[78]

The authors regard this undertaking, in the case of the Polish peasants, as having been primarily the task of leaders. The leaders had to prepare the peasantry (by stimulating and forming within them proper attitudes) for the acceptance of the new schemes of behavior. In the case of the Polish peasant, it was necessary to make use of attitudes responsible for the unity of the old primary group communities, in developing a sense of, and attachment to, a wider community on a national basis. Alongside of this absorption of the peasants in a wider group, the new schemes had to provide for the expression of new attitudes which could not secure such expression in old primary group communities. Both of these objectives were realized by the fostering of "conscious cooperation" leading to the formation of organized groups all over the country but united through a press and through formal organization.

Three remarks may be made relative to the scheme of social disorganization and reorganization which Thomas and Znaniecki have developed and applied to Polish peasant society. First, we discover again that their theory, while in no sense contradicted by their documentary materials, to a considerable extent orders and transcends this material. Second,

[77] Vol. II, 1303   [78] Vol. II, 1304

that the theory is exceedingly plausible and certainly is profound. Third, it has been presented in terms of abstract conceptions that suit it to application to other societies. While their theory could easily have been stated in other ways, their formulation in terms of certain concepts suggests the possibility of application to other groups—a comparison which the authors emphatically urge.

4. Personal Disorganization. Personal disorganization is spoken of as "a decrease of the individual's ability to organize his whole life for the efficient, progressive, and continuous realization of his fundamental interests."[79] Elsewhere, in referring to demoralization, the authors speak of it as "the decay of the personal life organization of an individual member of a social group."[80]

While personal disorganization is not coterminous with social disorganization, it usually implies such a state. It indicates generally that the rules and institutions do not correspond to the real attitudes of its members, and that the old social system is decaying so rapidly that a new social system cannot grow fast enough to keep pace with the decadence. The individual is without the means of constructing a life organization that will permit him to cope with the new values in his experience; without a scheme he becomes demoralized.

The authors explain this process more clearly as it takes place in many Polish immigrants in this country. The Polish peasant reared in a primary group setting, develops a personality which is very dependent, for the regulation of conduct, upon habit and upon the immediate suggestions from his milieu. In a new situation, such as is represented by his residence in this country, he does not have the preparation which would permit him to develop a "new life organization with such elements as abstract individualistic morality, re-

[79] Vol. II, 1128-29   [80] Vol. II, 1647

ligious mysticism and the legal and economic systems which he finds in America. In order to reorganize his life on a new basis, he needs a primary group as strong and coherent as the one he left in the old country."[81] This he is unlikely to find. Consequently, confronted as he is with strange values, and not having the means of developing schemes which are socially supported by primary group relations, he is likely to incur demoralization, and this disorganization is likely to become progressive.

> An immigrant of the first generation who becomes demoralized in any particular line—family life, economic relations, community relations— soon loses moral self-control in general, all his institutional attitudes are more or less dissolved.[82]

This process of degeneration becomes greater in the second generation, "both because the parents have less to give than they had received themselves in the line of social principles and emotions, and because the children brought up in American cities have more freedom and less respect for their parents."

The authors have discussed the disorganization of the Polish adult immigrant as it is shown in economic dependency, in a break of conjugal relations, and in murder; in the case of children, as it is manifested in the vagrancy and dishonesty of boys and in the sexual demoralization of girls.

What is most conspicuous in the case of the adult is the emergence of temperamental attitudes. With the breakdown or inapplicability of the old rules as he has known them, and with his inability to construct a new set of rational values which may give him guidance, he falls back on temperamental attitudes as a means of defining situations, but they do not allow a social definition; so he is unable to form a

[81] Vol. II, 1650   [82] Vol. II, 1651

new life organization and suffers a disintegration of his former character.

What stands out most in the case of children is the fact that they are "amoral" rather than disorganized, living without socially sanctioned rules rather than having suffered a breakdown of such rules.

The authors have endeavored to support their theory of personal disorganization in the case of the adult and the child by the use of court records and records of social agencies. These materials are not satisfactory as a testing of the theory but are helpful in giving one a concrete and so a more appreciable understanding of the theory.

Our discussion of the authors' theories of personality and of disorganization does not do justice to the detail with which they are presented in the text. The discussion will suffice, however, to give a picture of the chief features of the theories and to show how they stem from the central view as to the relation between attitudes and values. While, as we have pointed out, materials in the form of documents are introduced in connection with the theories, thus permitting some concrete evaluation of the theories, the authors think of the theories as being primarily hypothetical. They urge the application of the theories to bodies of data other than those on the Polish peasant, as a means of assaying their value.

GENERAL EVALUATION

To form a proper perspective of the study made by Thomas and Znaniecki, one must realize that it is not a mere monograph on Polish peasant society. It is primarily an attempt to lay the basis for scientific social research and for scientific social theory. This attempt is based on four considerations.

1. They desire to construct an approach that is adopted

to the character of life in a complex civilized society. Particularly, it must be suited to the study of social change and transformation since this feature is outstanding in such a society. Further, the approach must be such as to lead to social theory adequate for social control.

To appreciate this point, it should be realized that there may be forms of study which do not have this character. Indeed, much of present day social research, however scientifically imposing, is not suited to the study of a changing society. Further, much of it may yield findings and relations which are "precise" without being able to offer any knowledge as to *how to change or control these relations*. This indicates that such research is not being applied to the line of inquiry which the theoretical character of social life requires. The ultimate test of the validity of scientific knowledge is the ability to use it for purposes of social control.

A scheme for the scientific study of social life must be able to cope with the central character of social life, and must offer the possibility of yielding knowledge that can be used for the control of that social life. The authors have endeavored to construct such a scheme.

2. A second consideration is the need of an approach that fits the unique character of change or interaction as its occurs in the case of human social life. What is unique, according to Thomas and Znaniecki, is the presence of a subjective as well as an objective factor. The influence of any objective factor always is dependent on the selective receptivity and positive inclination of the person. And, correspondingly, the change of an objective factor (as far as its influence on persons is concerned) is dependent upon the application to it of a new point of view or orientation. It is this idea which, as we have seen, the authors have expressed in their declara-

tion that both objective setting and subjective experience must be taken into account in the study of social change. It is this idea which they have expressed in their basic concepts of attitude and value, and it is this idea which they have elaborated and extended to their methodological formula designed to yield "laws of social becoming."

It seems certain that this methodological formula is invalid and that the thought of securing "laws of becoming" by it is chimerical. Further, one may even question both the logical and methodological adequacy of the concepts of "attitude" and "value." These admissions, however, do not affect the validity of the general belief that social life involves the interaction of objective factors and subjective experience. This notion, indeed, is in accord with common sense; it might be expressed in the statement that an individual acts toward objects in terms of what they mean to him.

An adequate scheme for the study of human society must pay due attention to this subjective factor. This, Thomas and Znaniecki have consistently sought to do, by always keeping an eye on human experience. They regard approaches which ignore or omit this subjective factor and which merely study relations between objective factors as being necessarily deficient, and incapable of yielding adequate knowledge of social life. Such approaches, it should be noted, are very conspicuous in contemporary social research and are usually justified and fortified by assertions as to their objectivity and scientific character.

3. The third consideration springs from the one just mentioned. It is a realization of the need of devising means that will enable one to "catch" this subjective factor and study it in interaction with the objective factor. This is an inescapable need if one admits the role of the subjective factor.

The authors have faced the problem squarely. Their answer, as we have seen, is that the means are provided by "human documents." The human document as an account of human experience gives empirical data on the subjective factor. Further, it is an "objective" record, enabling others to have access to the data and permitting one to return always to them.

4. The final consideration is the realization of the need of a theoretical framework in order to study social life. An approach without a guiding scheme is no approach. In the case of their own scheme, it should be noted that it is constructed on the basis of the very factors which represent the uniqueness of social life and which logically constitute the fact of social change. These factors are the subjective and objective as they are involved in interaction. As we have seen, the authors have conceptualized these factors in their notion of attitudes and values, and, with these as the foundation stones, they have developed the theoretical framework which we have considered. Their interest, in other words, has been to develop a conceptual scheme that would permit one to handle analytically and abstractly concrete material on social life, and thus permit comparative studies of different societies.

It is with a methodological scheme organized around these considerations that Thomas and Znaniecki made their monographic study of Polish peasant society. The scheme is well organized on the logical and methodological sides; the authors show full familiarity with the logic of science and with the canons of scientific procedure.

The application of the scheme to the Polish peasant society is a trial—in the sense of both an exemplification and a test. The authors are engaged in a pioneer undertaking; they continually stress the need of comparable studies of other societies to verify the "laws" and generalizations arrived at in the study of the Polish peasant; and in their concluding remarks[83] they emphasize the tentative character of their method, their analyses, and their results.

In the absence of comparable studies of other societies which can serve as a test of the authors' generalizations and theories, we are not in a position to decide categorically on their truth or falsity. All that can be done is to consider critically the application of their methodological approach (their "standpoint and method") to the study of the Polish peasant society. Since this application centers in the analysis of an extensive body of materials by means of a series of theoretical schemes, our interest must be focused on this undertaking. As a result, we have to ignore consideration of the rich body of illuminating interpretations which the authors have made of the Polish peasant society.

The problem, then, which confronts us here is that of the relation between their materials and their theoretical analysis. This problem has arisen at a number of points in our previous discussion; here we must consider it again. It is a problem which lies at the heart of the authors' undertaking; and it is a problem which is central in all social research which seeks to get at the "subjective" factor by means of documentary material, for it is a problem, ultimately, as to whether social research into subjective experience can be made to be scientific.

As we have seen, Thomas and Znaniecki, cognizant of the need of getting material on the subjective factor, have advo-

[83] "Our work does not pretend to give any definite and universally valid sociological truths, nor to constitute a permanent model of sociological research; it merely claims to be a monograph, as nearly complete as possible under the circumstances, of a limited social group at a certain period of its evolution, which may suggest studies of other groups, more detailed and more perfect methodically, thus helping the investigation of modern living societies to rise above its present stage of journalistic impressionism, and preparing the ground for the determination of really exact general laws of human behavior." (Vol. II, 1822-23)

[73]

cated the use of "human documents," of which they regard the life record as the most perfect form. They have given a vast quantity of various human documents in their work. These documentary materials are admittedly not as satisfactory as they would wish, but were the best that they could secure. These materials are those on which their work is primarily based, in the sense that supposedly the theoretical analyses either arose out of them or were tested by them. What can be said on this point of their inductive character? How does one work with human documents? How does one analyze them and interpret them?

It seems quite clear that Thomas and Znaniecki did not derive all of their theoretical conceptions from the materials which are contained in their volumes or from similar materials which they did not put into their volumes. Perhaps not even the major theoretical conceptions were derived from them. Indeed, the major outlines are foreshadowed in the previous writings of Thomas. It is rather self-evident that the authors began their study of the Polish peasant with the rudiments of their primary theoretical schemes, built out of much experience with human beings, many reflections and observations on human conduct, and considerable appreciation of human nature. Only individuals with such experience and gifts could have made the stimulating and incisive interpretations that they have made. It is further self-evident that their *particular* interpretations of Polish peasant life were not formed solely from the materials they present; we have to assume that the familiarity with Polish peasant life which enabled their interpretations was made in a wide variety of ways. Thus, while there can be no question but that much of the theoretical conception of the authors came from handling the documents, it is also true that a large part of it did not.

[74]

This point, in itself, is not important, except that it explains why the theoretical conceptions in *The Polish Peasant* far exceed the materials. The authors have shown surprising liberality in making generalizations—generalizations which seem to be very good, but for which there are few if any data in the materials. Omitting this overload of generalization, the important question is whether the materials adequately test the generalizations (regardless of their source) which are being applied to the materials. As our previous discussion has pointed out, the answer is very inconclusive. Some interpretations, indeed, are borne out by the content of the documents, and sometimes the interpretations do not seem to be verified adequately; in both instances, of course, the materials are a test. Usually, however, one cannot say that the interpretation is either true or not true, even though it is distinctly plausible.

In instances of plausible interpretations, all that one can say is that the interpretation makes the materials more significant than they were and makes the theoretical interpretation more understandable and familiar than it was previously. Perhaps, this is all that one can expect or should expect in the interpretative analysis of human documentary material. It is just this which one finds to be true of *The Polish Peasant,* yet if the theoretical analysis of human documents either only can be, or should be, of this sort, it leaves behind a number of important considerations and problems.

1. First, it would mean, obviously, that the materials are not a decisive test of the theoretical interpretations. Yet, the fact that both the material and the interpretation acquire significance and understanding that they did not have before, seems to mean that it is not a mere case of the illustration of the theory.

2. Second, it would follow that the test of the validity of

such theory would have to come in other ways, such as in its internal consistency, in the character of its assumptions, in its relation to other theories, in its consistency with what seems to be "human," or in other kinds of data than those provided by human documents.

3. Third, it would seemingly imply that the essential function of human documents would be to provide human materials which would yield to a sensitive and inquiring mind hunches, insights, questions suitable for reflection, new perspectives, and new understandings.

These considerations seem to represent the way in which the authors have actually worked with their theoretical conceptions and their data. In the authors, we have two excellent minds with a rich experience with human beings, with a keen sensitivity to the human element in conduct, with some fundamental notions and interests, with a number of important problems, with a variety of hunches, with a lively curiosity and sense of inquiry, with a capacity for forming abstract concepts—two minds, of this sort, approaching voluminous accounts of human experience, mulling over them, reflecting on them, perceiving many things in them, relating these things to their background of experience, checking these things against one another, and charting all of them into a coherent abstract and analytical pattern. Perhaps, this is, after all, how the scientist works. At any rate, it is not surprising that out of such efforts, Thomas and Znaniecki should have produced such an impressive work as this analysis of Polish peasant society.

In the light of the general discussion of *The Polish Peasant*, some concluding thoughts may be given on the problem of the scientific analysis of human documents.

It seems clear that the meaningful content of such documents is dependent on the ideas, questions, and knowledge with which their analysis is undertaken. While this is true, obviously, in the understanding of any body of scientific materials, it seems to be more pronounced in the interpretation of records of human experience. Such a record is less self-evident as to its meaning. The implication is that, generally, the value of the analysis will depend on the experience, intelligence, skill, and fruitful questions of the student. As these factors vary, so will vary the interpretation. The person who has a broad acquaintance with human beings, who, as we say popularly, understands human nature, and who has an intimate familiarity with the area of experience that he is studying, should make a more able analysis than one who is less well equipped in these respects. This, of course, is to be expected. The point is worthy of mention here only to emphasize that the interpretative content of a human document depends markedly on the competence and theoretical framework with which the document is studied. One person, by virtue of his experience and his interests, may detect things in a document that another person would not see.

This flexibility of a document to interpretation would be of no importance if the document could be used as an effective test of the specific interpretation which is made of it, but it is at this point that difficulty enters. In the case of simple facts, the document may indeed prove or disprove an assertion made about it, but the closer one approaches to abstract interpretation the less satisfactory is the document as a test. Human documents seem to lend themselves readily to diverse interpretations. One can see this in the ease with which they can be analyzed by different theories of motivation. Theories seem to order the data.

The reasons for this condition may be sought, presumably, in a number of directions. One reason which readily suggests

[77]

itself is that the document may not be sufficiently thorough; what is needed is a fuller and more ample account of the experience which is interpreted. Many students of social research hold to this belief and, accordingly, have committed themselves to the meritorious task of securing "exhaustive" accounts. Thomas and Znaniecki have this idea in mind in advocating the use of "life histories." Theoretically, an exhaustive account which would present all details of an experience or series of experiences would serve as a decisive test of interpretation. Actually, such exhaustive accounts are not secured and, perhaps, never can be secured. In the case of accounts which are generally regarded as being full and detailed (as in the autobiography of Władek or in a psychoanalytic record), one still finds an inability of the account to test decisively most interpretations. The interpretation may be plausible and even self-evident to one who holds the theory from which the interpretation stems; to another who has a different theoretical framework, a different interpretation may seem to be more telling and true.

This suggests that the deficiency of human documents as a test of interpretation is due in large part to the nature of the act of interpretation. To interpret is to apply concepts or categories, and it seems that such interpretation in the instance of the human document, as in that of any human experience, is so much a matter of judgment that categories that are congenial and self-evident to one, readily fit the experience.[84] Perhaps, this need not always be true; it does seem, however, to represent the present status of the inter-

[84] Part of the difficulty comes from the fact that the categories employed are left undefined, or else are defined in an imprecise manner. Consequently, one is at a loss to identify details of experience that would permit one to determine whether or not the category fits. The application of the category is a matter of judicious judgment rather than of decisive test.

pretation of human experience, especially so, on the more abstract levels.

It would follow that the validation or invalidation of many theories and views has to be done by means other than the use of *specific experiences*. Such means as those of logical criticism, relation to other theories and bodies of fact, and the use of a mass of general experiences (as is done in supporting the theory of culture as against the doctrine of instinct) seem to be those which are commonly employed. Specific accounts of experience serve, apparently, only to make clear the nature of the interpretation. The point suggested here (as applied to human documents) may be stated extremely in the declaration that a document has value only in terms of the theory with which it is interpreted, but that the validity of the theory usually cannot be determined by the document.

One way in which students may attempt to test the interpretation of human documents is by the use of statistical procedure. This procedure would consist of the collection of a representative number of accounts and the determination of the proportion that show the given interpretation. This would be compared with a control group. Such a procedure, however, while methodologically sound, would be of no special value if the separate documents, whether of the study group or of the control group, could not be used as an effective test of the interpretation.

This whole situation suggests something in the nature of a dilemma. On one hand, the study of social life seems to require the understanding of the factor of human experience. This subjective aspect must be secured, as Thomas and Znaniecki show. Studies which confine themselves to "objective factors" remain inadequate and one-sided. Yet the identification of the human experience or subjective factor,

[79]

seemingly, is not made at present in ways which permit one to test crucially the interpretation. Identification and interpretation remain a matter of judgment. Their acceptance depends on their plausibility. At best, the materials only enable one to make out a *case* for the theoretical interpretation.

The inadequacy of human documents in testing interpretation is a primary reason why they are rejected by many as materials for scientific study. When one adds to this the fact that usually the separate document cannot very well stand evaluation according to the criteria of representativeness, adequacy, and reliability, it is easy to see why human documents become suspect as a scientific instrument. Yet to renounce their use in the scientific investigation of human life would be to commit a fatal blunder, for theoretically, they are indispensable and actually they may be of enormous value. The effective use which has been made of them by Thomas and Znaniecki is ample demonstration of this value.

A few concluding remarks may be made on this point. First, one should note that human documents may be very serviceable in aiding the student to acquire an intimate acquaintance with the kind of experience he is studying, in suggesting leads, in enabling insight, and in helping him to frame more fruitful questions. It is much better to develop one's theoretical judgments with the aid of such documents than to form them, speaking extremely, in a vacuum. The use of documents offers to the student the opportunity to increase his experience and to sharpen his sense of inquiry. Other things being equal, the student who develops through the use of documents an intimate acquaintance with an area of life will be able to analyze it more fruitfully than would one lacking such an acquaintance.

In a sense, human documents serve the reader of a report in the same way in which they serve the investigator. They permit him to form a closer acquaintance with the kind of experience which is being studied and to form a judgment as to the reasonable nature of the proposed interpretations. Admittedly, this judgment will vary with different readers; those who possess a facility in understanding human beings and who already have an intimate familiarity with the people being studied can make a better judgment than those lacking this facility and this intimate knowledge. Perhaps, only the judgments of those who are similar or superior in competence and familiarity to the investigator are significant in the critical evaluation of a report. Other readers would have to temper their own judgments by some acceptance, on authority, of the analysis which the investigator makes of human documents.

CONCLUSION

This report can be concluded with a listing of some of the more important contributions which have made *The Polish Peasant* meritorious and which explain the profound influence which it has had on sociology and social psychology.

1. A demonstration of the need of studying the subjective factor in social life.

2. The proposing of human documents as source material, particularly the life record, thus introducing what is known as the life history technique.

3. A statement of social theory which outlines the framework of a social psychology and the features of a sociology. The view of social psychology as the subjective aspect of culture has been particularly influential.

4. A statement of scientific method which has stimulated and reinforced the interest in making sociology a scientific discipline.

5. A number of important theories, such as that of per-

sonality, that of social control, that of disorganization, and that of the four wishes.

6. A variety of concepts which have gained wide acceptance, such as attitude, value, life organization, definition of situation, and the four wishes.

7. A rich content of insights, provocative generalizations, and shrewd observations.

8. An illuminating and telling characterization of the Polish peasant society.

What is perhaps of chief importance is the marked stimulation which it has given to actual social research.

COMMENT BY W. I. THOMAS

I find that Blumer's analysis of *The Polish Peasant* is a very profound, able, and salutary piece of work. Directed toward a study of considerable magnitude and rather extensive pretentions which represents, in my opinion, a fundamentally superior approach, the criticism shows the shortcomings and at the same time the merits of this work and prepares the way for improved procedure in future studies of social processes. It is my hope that this criticism will be published, for, while it is directed toward a specific performance, it has a general application and impresses me, in fact, as the best methodological contribution which has appeared in the field of social psychology.

Twenty years have passed since the publication of *The Polish Peasant* and in the meantime my views have naturally undergone considerable change and I know that the same is true of Znaniecki. As soon as I viewed the work as completed in print, and even before that point, I was considerably dissatisfied with it. I have since made a rather thoroughgoing criticism of it from my present standpoint in my seminary at Harvard and much of my criticism corresponds with that of Blumer. I will briefly indicate my present position on certain points.

It is true that the concrete materials of the volume are not adequately correlated with the methodological scheme. It is a fact that the methodological note in Volume One was prepared just before the first two volumes went to press. It was a combination of assumptions which I had made for several years in a course on "Social Attitudes" and some standpoints developed by Znaniecki in a volume in Polish on "Values." It was in the nature of an essay. It was influenced by our investigation but was not altogether the result of it and its claims were not systematically exemplified by the materials. It was as if we had done what we could with the present materials and then, or in the meantime, elaborated a series of hypotheses to be tested in further studies of nationalities and cultures.

In all scientific investigation, it is almost the rule that a promising initial undertaking is incorrect and incomplete at points but may open the way to the participation and corrective contributions of a considerable interest-group, as in the case of *The Polish Peasant.*

I approve our separation of attitudes and values, or psychological sets and tendencies to act, on the one hand, and the external stimuli to action on the other, and of our general description of the interaction of these factors, but I think we went too far in our confident assumption that we shall be able to lay bare the complete and invariable nature of this interaction and thus determine the *laws* of "social becoming."

In this connection, social scientists have been influenced by the history of the physical sciences where it has been possible to determine laws because the materials are stable. But human material is never stable. Individuals differ in their physiological constitutions and learned attitudes and the same individual differs at different moments. We have recognized this in a passage quoted by Blumer:

A social value, acting upon individual members of the group, produces a more or less different effect upon every one of them; and even when acting upon the same individual at various moments it does not influence him uniformly.

Nevertheless, there are certain general correspondences in human nature to begin with, and society by its institutions, teachings, rules, rewards, and penalties does establish a degree of regularity and probability. It is able to condition its material to a certain degree and secure, on the whole, expected behavior. We should therefore not speak of social *laws* but seek to establish high degrees of *probability* in the interaction of attitudes and values.

Blumer here, and others elsewhere, have criticized the "human document" as incomplete and unreliable, and this is correct in the sense that all human testimony and communication tend to be reserved, biased, and directed toward the production of desired attitudes in others. It is known also that even the most conscientious court testimony is often incomplete and unreliable because perception and memory do not register the data adequately.

Nevertheless, in every day life in forming decisions and regulating social interaction, we are forced to utilize the testimony of others, their representations of reality, just as the courts are forced to use sworn testimony. In spite of the fact that the representations are not completely reliable, they are indispensable. A social psychology without records of experience would be like a court without testimony.

The behavior document, whether autobiography, case record, or psychoanalytic exploration, is a more or less systematic record of individual experience, and the claim for the doc-

[84]

ument is that the extensive record of experience will reveal the general schematization of individual life. In a record of this kind, we are able to view, in their evolution, the behavior reactions in the various situations and crises, the emergence of personality traits, the determination of concrete acts, and the formation of life policies. A series of such records taken comparatively reveal certain regularities, sequences, and probabilities when taken in connection with specific experiences in specific situations.

Moreover, even a highly subjective, delusional, or fabricated document has significance, since it represents attitudes which may pass into action. I quote what I said in this connection in a later volume:

A document prepared by one compensating for a feeling of inferiority or elaborating a delusion of persecution is as far as possible from objective reality, but the subject's view of the situation, how he regards it, may be the most important element for interpretation. For his immediate behavior is closely related to his definition of the situation, which may be in terms of objective reality or in terms of a subjective appreciation—'as if' it were so. Very often it is the wide discrepancy between the situation as it seems to others and the situation as it seems to the individual that brings about the overt behavior. To take an extreme example, the warden of a New York prison recently refused to honor the order of the court to send an inmate outside the prison walls for some specific purpose. He excused himself on the ground that the man was too dangerous. He had killed more than one person who had the unfortunate habit of talking to himself on the street. From the movement of their lips, he imagined they were calling him vile names, and he behaved as if this were true. If men define situations as real, they are real in their consequences.

Now the behavior record may be viewed and applied in several ways. In *The Polish Peasant*, the main line of inquiry was concerned with the problem of immigration and the changing attitudes and values in the movement of hundreds of thousands of the members of one cultural group into another cultural group, viewed in terms of individual and group organization and disorganization. At the same time,

[85]

we had in mind the bearing of the results of this specific investigation on social problems in general. In this connection, an uncritical use of copious documents was sufficient to reach certain important results. For example, we used letters exchanged between immigrants in America and their families in Poland, some of them in series extending over twenty years, and while there was much fabrication in the correspondence, it revealed striking changes in attitudes and values.

That is to say, our procedure and materials were relatively adequate for the determination of lines of social change in a block of population in transition from an agrarian to an industrial phase and from one milieu to another, but in other connections, and especially in the treatment of behavior irregularities as shown in delinquency, crime, and psychopathic trends, it is important to have, in addition to the narrative of the subject, the testimony of family members, teachers, neighbors, etc. Thus, the behavior records of the child clinics are contributing important data by including the child's account of the difficult situation, the often conflicting definition of this situation given by parents, teachers, etc., and the recording of such facts as can be verified about the situation by disinterested investigators. The criminological and psychopathic records in Sweden are particularly good because the state is able, so to speak, to compel the participation of outsiders, including employers, and the narrative of the subject is obtained more than once and at different times by different persons.

In our study, we did not associate statistical methods and controls with our documents. This would have been difficult in view of the character of the materials, which for the most part were found ready made and were not systematically prepared. But this was a defect of our method and materials and it is evident that what is needed in the study of social change and of individual adjustment and maladjustment is both the continued collection of the life records of normal, pathological, criminal, inferior, and superior individuals in our own and other nationalities and cultures and the application of appropriate statistical studies as a basis for the inferences drawn. And these inferences in turn must be continually subjected to further statistical analysis as it becomes possible to transmute more factors into quantitative form. Statistics become, then, the continuous process of verification and of hypothesis formation.

In the same connection, it is evident that statistical studies of the behavior of populations will have a limited meaning so long as the statistical data are not supplemented by individual case histories.

COMMENT BY FLORIAN ZNANIECKI

I share unreservedly the opinion of Thomas about the superior merit of Blumer's critical analysis of *The Polish Peasant*. However, I am rather more optimistic than Blumer seems to be—or perhaps only less circumspect—concerning the possibility of utilizing the data of active human experience, accessible mainly through verbal communication, oral or written, as a basis for objectively verifiable scientific theory. The better I realize the deficiencies of our attempt, the more clearly I see that these deficiencies may be corrected in future attempts.

In one respect *The Polish Peasant* has apparently achieved some degree of recognized theoretic validity—of a kind. As a *sociographic* study, i.e., a synthetic description of a particular human collectivity, it seems to have advanced the conceptual knowledge of this collectivity.

Blumer justly points out that in interpreting our materials

[87]

we have made use of a considerable body of previously acquired knowledge concerning the Polish peasant class as a part of the total Polish society during a certain period of its existence. No investigator who did not possess this knowledge could have drawn from our material all the conclusions we have reached. But is it not the same in every kind of research that is dealing with concrete complexities of interconnected empirical data? Is not, say, a geographer who has previous knowledge about a certain area capable of inducing from his observations of newly discovered data within this area such inferences as no other geographer, equally competent but lacking that knowledge, could draw? This knowledge which we have assimilated and used to throw additional light upon our documents was not mere personal acquaintance with the facts, such as is derived from active participation in a collectivity. It was conceptual knowledge, the result of previous methodical studies made by Polish historians, anthropologists, ethnographers, economists. Perhaps we were not explicit enough in giving all the credit that was due to our predecessors. A bibliography added to the text would have obviated this deficiency. But as the work was intended for American readers, this did not seem indispensable, especially since none of our predecessors in this field had used the kind of material and applied the kind of method we did.

Now, the decisive question in this respect is whether in any research of this monographic type new concrete data investigated with the help of previous conceptual knowledge lead to new conceptual knowledge or not. If so, then the new knowledge must be inductively derived from the new data. As far as *The Polish Peasant* is concerned, there is unanimous opinion among students of Polish peasant life who have read it that it does bring new knowledge. I can refer to such authorities as F. Bujak, professor in Lwow, W.

Staniewicz, professor in Wilno, former minister of agrarian reform, and the late W. Grabski, erstwhile prime minister. Grabski, who had given some valuable advice to Thomas twenty-six years ago, wrote two years ago that *The Polish Peasant* is the first and basic work in the sociology of Polish rural life. At this very time, the main conclusions of this work are being used as premises for new intensive research that is carried on by the State Institute for Rural Culture in Warsaw.[85] Further, it apparently helps in the understanding of the new evolutionary processes that have occurred during the twenty years since its publication, both among the peasants in Poland and among the immigrants in America. Finally, it seems to be of some indirect assistance in shaping the policy of the Polish government in matters of rural education and agrarian reform.

However, granted that our work has enlarged by inductive methods the preexisting set of conceptual knowledge about the Polish peasant class, this point, though not altogether irrelevant to the main problem of Blumer's discussion, is of secondary significance, for the criteria of validity by which this type of knowledge is estimated are essentially the same as those applied in historical or anthropological monographs. And in the series of methodological discussions initiated by the Social Science Research Council these criteria are as much under indictment as those of general sociology, theoretic economics, comparative linguistics—if not more so. For the sociographer or the historian, in analyzing a particular concrete collectivity at a particular period of its duration, uses general sociological concepts. The validity of the final synthesis depends largely (though not exclusively) on the validity

[85] Dr. Joseph Chalasinski, Director of the Institute, has made this clear in his four-volume study *The Young Generation of Peasants*, published a few months ago.

of that abstract, comparative knowledge which these concepts embody. And there is no doubt that much of the latter represents the result of methodically defective reflection about social phenomena: it belongs to that "common-sense sociology" which is at least forty centuries old and has grown rather than improved with age.

The Polish Peasant claims to be, not mere sociography, but at least a fragmentary and tentative contribution to sociology, viewed as an inductive, analytic, classificatory and nomothetic science. This is the claim which Blumer has mainly subjected to his penetrating criticism.

Here again let us begin by settling one fundamental question. In so far as we ever conveyed the impression that our sociological theories were exclusively founded on induction from the data that were at our disposal in the form in which we had obtained them, we were indisputably in the wrong. Blumer is right in stating that, besides particular knowledge of Polish society mentioned above, we have brought to bear upon our data previous results of comparative analysis and generalization. Thomas had at the time already formulated several well known and original theories in social psychology and sociology, based upon an exceptionally great mass and variety of significant data carefully chosen from many different cultures; and in starting to collect materials concerning European peasants he meant to apply his theories to this new mass of data. I had published several works in general theory of culture and in epistemology which eventually proved to have some bearing, however abstract and indirect; the former upon the data of Polish peasant culture, the latter on the method of handling them. Furthermore, both of us had been more or less, though differently, influenced by various classical works in sociology and the neighboring fields.

All this, however, is surely no argument against the inductive character of our work—nor does Blumer mean it as a reproach. For he knows as well as any methodologist that no inductive science ever draws valid theory directly and exclusively from facts as they are given in naïve observation, undirected and unrelated to previous theory. A fact is theoretically significant—is, indeed, a fact at all in the scientific sense—only if it serves either to raise a problem or to solve a problem. The former happens when a ready hypothesis is applied to it; the latter when a new hypothesis is based upon it.

In *The Polish Peasant* we did try to proceed as all inductive science proceeds: we raised problems by applying hypotheses to our facts, and we solved problems by formulating hypotheses based on our facts. We may have yielded too often to the common temptation of assuming that our ready hypotheses solved the problems raised by their application to new facts, instead of always deliberately seeking for such facts or such aspects of facts as would compel us to modify or supplement our hypotheses. Yet, whatever theories we had brought into our research from previous generalizations, our own or other people's, undoubtedly quite a number of new general problems and new hypotheses were the result of subsequent induction from our empirical data. In building those theories which Blumer mentions in his concluding remarks, we ought to have separated clearly that which was derived from other sources from that which was unmistakably founded on the data used in our work. Our failure to do so was due to the fact that we did not originally intend to build new theories, but simply to present a collection of human documents, with such comments and interpretations as would make their utilization by other scientists possible. Our theories—or rather whatever was new in them—grew slowly and gradually in the course of years, during the very process

[91]

of selecting, preparing, interpreting, analyzing, and organizing our materials.

And now comes the culminating question: What is the validity of these inductive sociological theories of ours as judged by the recognized standards of valid scientific induction? Blumer proves—and I fully agree with him—that our theories have not been adequately tested by our facts, as testing is understood in more advanced sciences. But, after having exposed the weakness of our heuristic categories as instruments for building theory from empirical material, he ends by making the very nature of our material largely responsible for our failure to satisfy the demand of scientific validity in testing theories by facts. This brings him to the dilemma stated on pp. 79-80: "On the one hand, the study of social life seems to require the understanding of the factor of human experience. This subjective aspect must be secured. . . . Yet the identification of the human experience or subjective factor, seemingly, is not made at present in ways which permit one to test crucially the interpretation. Identification and interpretation remain a matter of judgment." Though this conclusion is very carefully worded and may be taken as referring only to the present stage in the development of social science, yet because no way is shown out of the dilemma, it does suggest that the need of relying on personal insight rather than standardized common experience in dealing with human data is fundamental and not temporary.

Such a generalization does not follow from the critical analysis of *The Polish Peasant;* for it seems to me that, whatever arbitrariness there is in our interpretation of our materials as bearing upon our theories, is entirely explicable by the inadequacy of that general conceptual framework with which we have approached our data. I refer to the excessive simplicity of the "attitude-value" conceptual combination—

that simplicity which made it so popular and so dangerous to use.

I do not think there is anything essentially wrong with either of these concepts as general categories embracing the primary objects and the primary forces of empirical human reality (though for several reasons I prefer now to use "tendency" instead of "attitude"). You can always *designate* a value or an attitude as a particular component of an individual's active experience, if this individual communicates to you his experience symbolically or if you infer it from his outward behavior; and your designation will enable other observers who have the same sources of information to identify this value or attitude. Nor is there any difficulty about distinguishing empirically values from attitudes, as long as these categories are kept logically distinct. The meaning of a value need never be confused with an attitude toward this value, for it does not consist in the bearing of this value upon the agent but in its bearing upon other values actually or potentially experienced by him. The meaning of a word is its symbolic reference to the objects it designates, whereas an attitude toward this word is, e.g., its appreciation as high or low, sacred or profane. My attitude of hate toward an enemy is not a part of his meaning: the latter consists in his having hurt, or being presumably able and willing to hurt, some positive values of mine. If I am a true Christian, my attitude toward him will not be hate but love, though his meaning may be still that of an enemy.

The difficulty lies elsewhere. You cannot *define* any particular value or any particular attitude you have designated. It is impossible to determine objectively its essential characteristics, for as a concrete component of human active experience it is *infinitely variable*. Whereas in *The Polish Peasant* we have treated both as if they were stable *elements* of the human world, fit to be defined and classified in abstract isolation from other elements—just as, say, the substantial "bodies" and the absolute movements of older physical theories.

It took me many years to realize this methodological error of ours, which is the more puzzling as we did not apply our conception consistently throughout the work. As Blumer points out, we have made very little use of the causal formulas which logically resulted from it (the "value-attitude-value" and "attitude-value-attitude" schemes). And we have used other basic concepts, such as "rule," "institution," "organization," which are logically irreducible to our two fundamental categories.

I believe I understand now the original source of our inadequate categorization. The general problem we tried to solve was the problem of *change*. Now, change presupposes *stability*—and we took stability for granted. We failed to see that in the world of culture, stability is the primary and the more difficult problem, for viewed as a concrete world of active experience of billions of individuals coming and going through thousands of generations, it is in ceaseless and apparently chaotic flux. We may well be excused, indeed, for all sciences have begun by assuming that reality is basically stable and only changes need explanation. The Heraclitean conception was, and still remains, a metaphysical belief rather than a genuine and working methodological postulate in most fields of scientific research. Even physics has taken three centuries from the time it first glimpsed the possibility of its application until it realized fully this possibility.

Now, if you take stability for granted, you begin by assuming simply and naïvely that the entities that are given to you in superficial observation or constructed by you in realistic symbolization—earth and water, heavenly bodies, plants and animals, temples and paintings, myths and languages, families and cities, states and societies, factories and banks—are substantial realities, essentially enduring and only accidentally changing. Then you may go beyond this stage and recognize change as resulting from, though not inherent in, the essence of reality, conceiving those entities as variable secondary combinations of primarily stable elements. This is what we tried to do, and I think it was better than what many sociologists had been doing and some are doing still. We were not prepared to find that there was no stability even in our elements—that there is no original, substantial stability anywhere in the social world either in the "objective environment" of man or in the "subjective disposition" of man. How many students of culture and mankind are ready even now, not merely to grant this idea in the abstract, but to *use* it consistently as instrumental, heuristic premise in stating their problems and formulating their hypotheses?

What does, indeed, such an idea imply in terms of scientific method in the field of sociology? It implies that duration, uniformity, repetition must be sought, if they are to be found at all, not in the nature of things, not in human nature, but in some kind of dynamic order—or orders—into which infinitely variable data of human experience and active human tendencies are made to fit, become standardized, regulated and organized. If there is to be social science, methodical observation must reconstruct these orders, methodical induction analyze them, compare, classify and explain. And they can do it.

These are some of the considerations which have made me adopt finally the concepts of *system* and *pattern* as heuristic sociological categories. These concepts, if not these terms, are derived from other sciences, and sociologists have used them extensively for years. We really used them in *The Polish*

[95]

Peasant, e.g. in our theory of the family as a group, in our studies of organization and disorganization, and in other parts of the work. Of course, to have these concepts truly useful as instruments of scientific research, they must be made explicit, exact, and complete. This is not the place to discuss them. Consider only what bearing their use has in a specific instance upon the main problem under discussion in Blumer's analysis.

Take a kind of complex social datum which has been many times treated in *The Polish Peasant:* a conjugal relation. If reduced (as we assumed we were doing) to a combination of elementary attitudes and values of the two individuals, every one to be defined separately with the help of letters, autobiographic statements or other human documents, no two observers would agree as to what constituted it. But if it is heuristically assumed to be an organized system of socially standardized values and normatively regulated active tendencies, each definable only with reference to the system as a whole in so far as standardized or regulated, then our task of reconstructing it objectively becomes incomparably more hopeful, but also more exacting.

We shall need extensive records of the whole history of the relation as experienced and acted by both partners. Diaries, letters, autobiographies of husband and wife would supply the necessary material, supplemented and controlled if possible by statements of observers. Half a dozen investigators, studying this material independently, may still disagree in the interpretation of much, perhaps most, of it. But if they share the common theoretic purpose of discovering whatever dynamic order there may be in this fluid complexity of the active experiences of two people living together through a number of years, there will be a core, however small, of data they will all consider as objectively established.

[96]

They will find, for instance, that both husband and wife consider themselves and each other lastingly bound together by a set of common values which each experiences somewhat differently from the other and variously at various moments of his or her life, but which to both possess a certain practically standardized content and meaning from which their experiences seldom deviate in a marked way, and if they do, the deviation is either ignored, considered as irrelevant, or ruled away, regarded as illusory or wrong. The "sacrament" of marriage as a religious value, the home, common property, children, may be such bonds. It will be found further that the husband considers himself and is considered by his wife, morally obliged to perform certain kinds of actions, and to abstain from other kinds of actions, and vice versa. There will be evidence that both have frequently tended to follow such norms, though these tendencies have not been always active when they were expected to be, or were often manifested only in words, while many actions conflicting with the norms were performed. In short, our investigators will reach a certain minimum of theoretically standardized factual information concerning some practically standardized values and normatively regulated active tendencies which constitute the nucleus of this particular conjugal relation as a social system.

But this is only the first step. Our reconstruction of this system is still in some measure conjectural and presumably incomplete. It will become more and more certain and more and more complete if we discover by similar methods that this particular conjugal relation follows a certain pattern which it shares with other conjugal relations, notwithstanding individual variations and deviations. And a still greater certainty will be reached if each of these conjugal relations is found to be part of a more comprehensive social order, such

[97]

as the family or kinship group, and is interdependent with other social relations, also following specific, more or less general, patterns.

Only then, with reference to such dynamic systems, which represent the only form of stability existing in the social world or the cultural world at large, can problems of change be adequately put and solved.

To summarize: social data, as accessible chiefly through communication, preferably embodied in human documents, can be valid tests of sociological theory because, and, in so far as, they are not isolated but belong to a practical social order, not realized by the agency of the investigator, though empirically accessible to him. Sociology, with other inductive sciences, has two objective tests of its validity: logical coherence of its theories and factual coherence of the reality upon which its theories bear. The latter is not dependent on the former, is not an ideal product of theoretic thinking, but a real order compelling methodical observation to follow it in reconstructing the facts. But, of course, only *methodical* observation is compelled to follow it; and methodical observation presupposes previous theoretic thinking and serves new theoretic thinking. No method has been yet devised in any science that can render thought unnecessary; and thought is, after all, personal, human activity.

Part Two

Proceedings of the Conference
on
Blumer's Analysis

Part Two

Transcript of the Conference Proceedings

The Conference called by the Committee on Appraisal of Social Research convened in the Social Science Research Council offices at 230 Park Avenue, New York City, on December 10, 1938, at 9:55 A.M.

Those present were: Gordon W. Allport, Read Bain, Herbert Blumer, F. W. Coker, Max Lerner, George P. Murdock, Roy F. Nichols, E. G. Nourse, A. T. Poffenberger, Samuel A. Stouffer, W. I. Thomas, Warren S. Thompson, Willard W. Waller, Malcolm M. Willey, Louis Wirth, Donald Young.

CHAIRMAN THOMPSON: I will make a very brief statement regarding the purpose of the Committee. The people who wanted it established, and in particular our chairman, Mr. Day, felt that there is a definite need for finding out what is significant work in social science and how it is done.

The Committee decided to ask certain men to make appraisals of particular pieces of work in sociology, history, political science, anthropology, and economics, and to be guided in such appraisals by three general questions. First, What was the purpose of the author in this particular piece of work? It was hoped that the answer to this question would not only bring to light secondary purposes of the author which might be fully as important for social science as his own primary purpose but would also help in answering the second question which was considered the most important of the three, namely, How successful has the author been in the achievement of his purpose? The consideration of this question would naturally involve an appraisal of the adequacy of data used and the methods employed for the problem in hand. How far were the data and the methods employed? How far could they be useful in other research in this field?

The third general question was, What generalizations, if any, were reached and do they appear to be sound deductions from the data presented? If there are any recommendations for social action, are they proper conclusions from the data?

Mr. Blumer addressed himself to these questions, as you will recognize, in the work that he has done here, but it was hoped that this conference might raise many questions and bring out many aspects of what is significant research in social science.

Now I might just say a very brief word about how the particular pieces of work were selected for appraisal. The different members of the Committee canvassed a number of men in each field, sociology, anthropology, political science, history, and economics, and got statements from them regarding what they considered the most significant piece of work in their field which had appeared since the World War. We limited it to America and to the period since the war simply to keep within a certain definite era; whether that was wise or not, we are not sure, but that was what was done. It just happened that the first appraisal, I believe, to come in was this one on *The Polish Peasant*. Therefore, it was selected as the one on which to hold a conference and to try to make some further progress in appraising research in social science. Mr. Nourse, do you have anything to add?

MR. NOURSE: Nothing, except that every member of the Committee felt Blumer's report on *The Polish Peasant* was so good that while we are waiting for the others we should take this one for discussion by a group in sociology and related fields.

CHAIRMAN THOMPSON: Mr. Coker, do you have anything to add?

MR. COKER: No, I have nothing to add.

CHAIRMAN THOMPSON: We will proceed then. Mr. Thomas has kindly consented to make a brief statement regarding the origin and development of *The Polish Peasant*.

MR. THOMAS: The question of why and how I undertook this work and the difficulties of securing the materials may be of some interest now. My statement must be somewhat autobiographical to begin with.

Before I entered the University of Chicago as a graduate student in 1893, I had spent two semesters in Germany studying philology. At that time also, I became interested in the *Völkerpsychologie* represented by Lazarus and Steinthal. I had also been strongly impressed by Spencer's *Sociology*.

At that time, immigration was a burning question. About a million immigrants were coming here annually, and this was mainly the newer immigration, from southern and eastern Europe. The larger groups were Poles, Italians, and Jews. When I became a member of the faculty at Chicago, I gave, among other courses, one on immigration and one on social attitudes, and eventually I decided to study an immigrant group in Europe and America to determine as far as possible what relation their home mores and norms had to their adjustment and maladjustment in America.

In 1908, I had a conversation with Miss Helen Culver, heiress of the Mr. Hull who endowed the Hull House in Chicago with which Jane Addams was associated, and Miss Culver agreed to support the study to the amount of $50,000.

I was now in a difficult position. I had the money and the hunch, but I had no assurance that adequate materials on the immigrant groups would be accessible in Europe. I expected to find in the numerous journals of folklore rich materials on the peasant, but I soon found that these materials were of no value. They dealt with such things as the coloring of Easter eggs, figures in weaving, hedges, plows, outhouses, magical practices, etc. It was evident that I had to find other sources.

After a year's exploration, I decided to study the Poles, largely because I found there abundant materials, of a kind. In 1863, a Mr. Prószyński had established a weekly journal, the *Gazeta Świąteczna,* for the benefit and enlightenment of the peasants. It was a feature of a general movement for enlightenment carried on by the aristocracy and better classes. Following numerous revolts against Russia in which they had been cruelly crushed, the upper classes began to turn to the peasant as the hope of the country and to educate and idealize him. This went so far that the upper classes, particularly the artists, in some cases married peasant women. In this connection, the *Gazeta* played a prominent role. The peasants began to write to this journal all sorts of letters on all sorts of questions. I purchased the files of this journal covering the last twenty years, and this was one of the main sources of our European data. At the same time, during eight periods of residence in Poland, I collected about 8000 documents or items, altogether.

Another reason for my choice of the Poles was their behavior in America. They were the most incomprehensible and perhaps the most disorganized of all the immigrant groups. This may be illustrated by what the American police call "Polish warfare." A policeman might enter a saloon where there was a noisy crowd of Poles and say, "You men be quiet," and they might subside immediately or one of them might draw a gun and kill him. This was due to the fact that the Pole in America has two attitudes toward authority. One of these reflects the old peasant subordination to authority. They were called "cattle" by the landlords and submitted like cattle. The other attitude reflects the conception that there are no limits to the boasted American "freedom."

The greatest chagrin encountered in the course of the study was the loss of about one third of our materials. I was viewed with a great deal of suspicion by prominent Poles, because, while they claimed to be, and were, an oppressed minority, their oppression of the Ruthenians in Austrian Poland was more ferocious than their own oppression in Russian Poland. In this connection, a good many important documents, especially manuscripts, were withheld from me. Eventually, however, they thought better of it and sent a communication to me in Chicago that if I would come or send a representative, I could have everything. I sent an assistant, Mr. Kulikowski, who copied selected manuscripts and secured other materials which had not been revealed to me, and also the earlier files of the *Gazeta,* of which only two sets were in existence. At this point, however, the war intervened and Kulikowski, fleeing conscription, lost the material in Vilna. I have speculated on how much difference in our final results this loss meant, but on the whole I do not think it was very much.

Kulikowski was lost with the materials for a time, but very fortunately for me, Znaniecki appeared in Chicago quite unexpectedly. He was a brilliant young philosopher who represented also the Polish policy of promoting scholarship in the absence of a state and of institutions of learning. Learning and art were patronized extensively by the great estate owners and others and this was done in part by giving eminent and promising men some civic duties while they pursued their studies. At any rate, Znaniecki was in charge of a Bureau for the Protection of Emigrants, which meant advising all who planned to emigrate as to desirable destinations and guarding them against exploitation, especially in South America. Incidentally, it meant also, as I understood it, keeping the best elements in Poland and facilitating the departure of the remainder.

In this connection, Znaniecki had a wide experience with peasants both through interviews in his office and through frequent trips to their villages, and a very great deal of what Blumer appreciates as insight shown in the volumes, and of the general conceptual scheme, is due to Znaniecki's philosophical training and his experience with peasant life. I had talked with him in Poland and he had given me some documents. He came to America to promote the translation of Polish scientific works, perhaps also to look into what representations I was making of Poland, but war was declared on the day he sailed, and he remained here and worked with me for five years. So I considered that what I had lost through the war on the one hand, I had more than gained on the other.

CHAIRMAN THOMPSON: Before opening the general discussion, I will ask Mr. Blumer to sum up as briefly as he can what he considers the main points of his critique—just to freshen it in our minds.

MR. BLUMER: Mr. Chairman, I will be very brief. I will indicate the leading premises which I judged to underlie *The Polish Peasant*. The authors strongly emphasize the need of a plan of research that will be suited to a complicated changing society. They chose the Polish peasant culture as an in- instance of such a society and, consequently, the scheme which they propose may be taken as one that can be used to study any society which is undergoing change and transition.

Another premise that is fundamental to the whole work is their quite unvarnished declaration that the understanding of human life necessitates the grasping of what they term the subjective factor. The point here is, that in the study of human beings, one cannot confine one's self to a mere designation of the external factors which are playing upon such human beings and, subsequently, a designation of the kinds of reactions which these human beings make to these factors. Rather, one has to take into consideration the kind of selective tendency or disposition which these human beings have which determines the way in which they are going to react to these external influences playing upon them. As the authors have stated, it is necessary to take into account what they term *social value,* which corresponds roughly to these external factors, and what they term *attitude,* which corresponds to this subjective or internal aspect of human experience.

The declaration, then, is that the way in which human beings respond to what affects them is dependent upon the way in which they interpret these external factors. It becomes necessary, then, in organizing the scheme for studying human conduct to include these external factors designated as *values,* and the human factors of experience designated as *attitudes.* They propose to apply a scheme of research and social theory organized around these two basic factors of *attitude* and *value* to the Polish peasant society as a concrete instance.

To carry out their intention, two things are necessary. First, to develop a guiding theoretical scheme which will set hypotheses—which will provide a framework inside of which interpretation and analysis is to be carried on. Thomas and Znaniecki, in my judgment, have done this. All of their theories are developed in intrinsic relation to these basic conceptions of *attitude* and *value*. Whether they are analyzing the social organization of the peasant society, whether they are trying to construct, as they do, a theory of personality, whether they are seeking to explain social or personal disorganization, their theoretical scheme is always thoroughly coherent with these basic conceptions of the subjective disposition and the objective factor.

Secondly, to apply their scheme to the study of Polish peasant society, it becomes necessary to secure source data that will reveal this subjective factor in human experience and which, at the same time, will meet the usual requirements for scientific data, viz., that one can always go back to these data and that other workers may have access to them. In the effort to get data that would reveal this subjective factor, they depended upon *human documents,* or records of human experiences.

In *The Polish Peasant,* they present a number of different kinds of documents. The largest and most frequent type is letters. They present in the text some 700-odd letters that had been written by members of immigrant families to one another. A second kind of human document which they employ is the lengthy autobiography. They introduce only one in the text, though presumably they had others. The third type consists of local newspaper correspondence. Use was also made of the records of social agencies, of court records, and, in a few instances, of church and parish records. These, then, cover essentially the human documents with which they were working.

Thomas and Znaniecki have presented theories covering many topics, covering an enormously wide field, and the implication is that they have sought to demonstrate the validity of these theories by the use of this human documentary material. As I saw it, my task was to see to what extent this is true, and to this point I limited my appraisal. I did not seek to make any evaluation of the, to my judgment, very extensive, profound, and enlightening interpretation which Thomas and Znaniecki have made of the Polish peasant. I was interested specifically in how far one could go in evaluating the relation of the documents to the theoretical claims of the authors. This gave rise to a series of considerations which I will summarize very briefly.

I concluded that it is inconceivable that the theoretical schemes which Thomas and Znaniecki presented in their work could have been derived from their documentary materials. To put the matter graphically, if one should take the most intelligent person one could find, one with a flair for understanding human behavior, and present him with all the documentary materials in *The Polish Peasant* and ask him to make out of them as much as he could, giving him as much time as he wanted, I am quite positive that whatever he might produce in the way of theory would be pitifully weak and meager in comparison with the theories and interpretations of these documents presented by Thomas and Znaniecki. What does this signify? To me, it signifies that Thomas and Znaniecki have arrived at their theoretical schemes and interpretations in a large measure apart from the documentary materials with which they were working. I suspect that the major features of these theoretical schemes were developing in the mind of Mr. Thomas throughout the whole period of his life to which he has just referred. To the extent that this is true, one cannot declare that the theoretical views in *The Polish Peasant* arise solely from the materials, although clearly they do arise in part from the materials. However, the point is not very important because it does not matter much where or how a person gets his theoretical views. The only thing that matters is whether these theoretical views can be tested by the evidence submitted. This, then, became my task, to see to what extent this was true in this particular case.

My impression is that the larger part of their theoretical interpretation, and particularly its more abstract features, cannot be tested by their documentary materials. Instead, I found Thomas and Znaniecki presenting a document and making comments on it in the nature of an analysis. These comments are usually exciting and very plausible, but there is nothing in the nature of the document which enables one to declare whether or not their analysis is correct. This raises a fundamental question, viz., can the human document be used effectively as an indicative device, indicative in the sense of actually testing some theoretical assertion made with reference to it?

There is no question that when one applies these theoretical views to the documents, the documents become more meaningful—they give us a certain understanding which we do not have before the application of the theory. There is, furthermore, no question that this application makes the theoretical conceptions more meaningful and makes them easier to grasp. At the same time, that relationship does not, in my judgment, represent any validation of the theoretical conceptions themselves.

This raises the question of the use of human documents in sociological research, a question which transcends this particular monograph. I feel that one can apply any theoretical view to some specific human experience and gain a certain modicum of verification—not verification, but apparent substantiation of that theory. The point here, again, is that the human document does not seem to be crucial in determining the validity of the theory.

What I suspect, then, is that actually the documents were

used as a means of broadening the authors' experience, of providing them with a wide variety of leads and hunches, of enabling them to get a better understanding of the particular groups of people with which they were dealing, and were thus exceedingly fruitful devices. I repeat again, however, that I do not think the documents can be regarded as effective tests of the theoretical conceptions which the authors have presented.

I am going to conclude, Mr. Chairman, with a statement that may be a little extreme but may set the problem for discussion. My own feeling is that this work of Thomas and Znaniecki presents a dilemma as far as social research goes. My judgment is that it conclusively shows the need of recognizing and considering the subjective factor in human experience. It is also true, however, that the effort to study this subjective factor by the use of human documents is attended by enormous difficulty, primarily in that the documents do not seem to be an effective test of the theoretical ideas one may develop regarding human or group behavior. So the dilemma presents itself in this form: on one hand, an inescapable need of including the subjective element of human experience, but, on the other hand, an enormous, and so far, unsurmounted, difficulty in securing devices that will catch this element of human experience in the way that is customary for usable data in ordinary scientific procedure in other fields.

CHAIRMAN THOMPSON: It is open for discussion. I would rather not have to call upon individuals. Take your own course in this.

MR. LERNER: Could I ask Mr. Blumer a question? You use the concept, "validity of a social theory". For example, you say that these particular theories shed considerable illumination on the documents and upon the specific human experience embodied there. Now what is the test of the validity of a theory other than its capacity to shed considerable illumination upon the data?[1]

MR. BLUMER: You raise a question which I do not feel competent to answer. I do feel, however, that our theories are likely to undergo change, not as a result of being disproved, or by being applied to specific instances of behavior. I think they are likely to be tested, i.e., accepted or rejected, in terms of their application to a much broader variety of things. One is likely to accept or reject them in terms of how well they fit in with other points of view or theories which one holds. They are likely to be accepted or rejected in terms of their logical character, or consistency with premises upon which they seem to be based, and they also are likely to be accepted or rejected in terms of how well they seem to cover a general rather than a specific area of human experience and behavior.

To illustrate these rather vague remarks, one might take the doctrine of instincts. I think it would be possible to take almost any human document and interpret it to the satisfaction of one committed to the doctrine of instincts. Yet we do know that the doctrine of instincts is subject to enormous and perhaps rather valid criticism. That criticism does not emerge, as I see it, from specific accounts of behavior, but rather emerges from broad general considerations. I think, aside from the possible influence of fashion, that probably the decline of the instinct doctrine today is due to these more or less broad general criticisms. The decline has not been, as I see it, from the submission of specific instances of human experience which challenge that doctrine.

MR. LERNER: What I am asking is whether the instinct

[1] The following discussion on verification of theory is supplemented somewhat by the remarks of G. W. Allport, George P. Murdock, and Malcolm M. Willey, at the conclusion of the transcript. These statements were prepared some weeks after the Conference was held.

doctrine did not also illuminate bodies of material to which it was applied? Partially, at least, the problem that arose with respect to the instinct theory was the problem of definition—of what you would call an instinct. The theory became unusable when it became terribly amorphous.

I am still very much puzzled by your whole approach because you are subjecting the work itself to criticism in terms of whether or not it produces valid social theories or social hypotheses and yet I find no statement in your manuscript which gives any notion of what you mean by validity other than a greater degree of illumination. It seems we should tackle the problem of what constitutes validity.

Now you say a valid theory would have to square with other doctrines, or be consistent with other theories. You have admitted that the authors make their own philosophical and methodological ends meet within their own book. Then you want the other kind of consistency, that it should square with other theories which in themselves may or may not be valid, and I suppose the test of their validity would be whether they square with these *Polish Peasant* theories, let us say. That leaves us very much up in the air, unless we can establish criteria that will give meaning to the term "validity of a theory."

MR. BLUMER: Your inquiry is very genuine and very pertinent, but my purpose in this analysis was not to indicate the criteria of validity, but merely to see whether the documents seemed to validate the theories which were used to interpret the documents. As a result of that effort, I was led to venture the belief that the validation or invalidation of theories of human behavior, particularly on the more abstract levels, does not seem to depend upon the use of particular accounts of human experience.

One has a situation here which is different from that in

the physical and biological sciences. In the latter case, it seems to me that the validation or invalidation of the theory always goes back to some specific facts, some specific instances of the behavior of the objects that are being studied. I looked upon the human document as such a specific event, a specific kind of behavior, a specific type of human experience. Hence, I have a feeling that there is a fundamental difference between human documents as source data, as crucial data, and the data of the biological and physical sciences.

In analyzing this work I could seldom say with any conviction, "Yes, this interpretation is true or is not true." The best I could say was, "Well, the interpretation which they give is very plausible." I frequently had the feeling that, even if the particular case to which they applied the interpretation had been entirely different, the intrinsic value of the interpretation would still be the same.

MR. ALLPORT: Do you feel that human documents are weaker in this respect than other social science data? Do you think that we are any better off with statistical studies? Are you implying that if we employ mass data, we have better grounds for our conceptualization?

MR. BLUMER: Frankly, I do not think they would be better. It seems to me we must face this point upon which Thomas and Znaniecki base their whole work, viz., the indispensable necessity of getting at the subjective element in our efforts to understand human behavior, whether it is individual or collective. I think the statistical approach will generally, though not necessarily, confine itself to what it calls objective factors, in other words, external influences playing upon human beings which can be counted, and responses which likewise can be counted. Thus, the statistical approach will tend to ignore this mediating factor of subjective experience which Thomas and Znaniecki emphasize as essential. For this reason, the statistical approach will tend to remain one-sided. If the statistician should ever grapple with the identification of this subjective factor, then we would have to face the same problem we are now discussing.

MR. STOUFFER: Mr. Blumer, with respect to Mr. Lerner's question, I was wondering why you did not mention prediction, or stress prediction, as at least one of the criteria by which validity can be determined?

MR. BLUMER: As I said before, I did not feel it was part of my task to discuss the criteria of validity. Were I doing so, of course I would have to discuss prediction. I think the most successful test would be the one that Mr. Thomas mentions in the book, viz., the effectiveness of the theory from the standpoint of controlling the data to which it refers. That would be the ultimate test, the pragmatic test, I suppose, but I do not want to be led into a discussion of criteria of validity.

MR. WALLER: From the point of view suggested by Mr. Stouffer, it does not matter at all whether the interpretation of a particular case is true or false provided that the interpretation is true of some case to come. That is, if that is actually the way it worked out, it would not matter that some of the materials were fictional or fabricated in some way. Other people might study the book and get certain possible interpretations which they thereafter would apply to cases as they arose. Somebody else studying the Polish peasant at a different time would get a wholly different set of people, a wholly different set of documents. They would find some documents somewhere to which any one of those interpretations could somehow be applied.

MR. STOUFFER: It seems to me that this use of the materials for getting ideas and insights, and so on, is a use which nobody could quarrel with, but that the real problem Mr.

Blumer has placed before us is how we are going to know that the theory which we propound is correct. It seems to me, as Mr. Thomas has suggested in his rejoinder to Mr. Blumer's criticisms, that one of the important tests is whether the theory works in similar situations. The role of the statistical procedures often may be very simple, viz., that of counting the number of situations in which the theory works and the number of situations in which it does not work. This is the basis of all prediction. If the first count greatly exceeds the latter, a probability statement, a prediction, may be made. This is certainly one of the important criteria of the validity of a theory.

MR. LERNER: Can you define the word "work" to mean anything more than the shedding of illumination upon a new situation? When you say can it be applied successfully to a new situation, which I gather to mean a new set of data, again we ask what you mean by "successfully" and what you mean by whether the thing "works." You have not only the quantitative question of how much illumination it sheds, but also the subjective question of whether it sheds illumination for Mr. X and not for Mr. Y. I would use the word "predict" for something involving a good deal more certainty than any kind of literary illumination can give. So I do not think we have advanced the problem of testing the validity of the theory any by talking about its application to new data unless we talk about what we mean by a successful application.

I think Mr. Blumer, having used the concept, "validation of a theory", cannot very well say, "I have no responsibility for saying what validity is," because any fruitful use of such a concept involves a facing of the problem of what we mean by validity.

MR. BLUMER: Well, in my discussion of Thomas' work, I

have used the term "validity" to refer to situations where an interpretation is proposed to apply to some specific account of experience. I ask myself, is that interpretation tested and can it be tested by that kind of an experience? In the light of that experience, is the interpretation true or is it not true?

MR. LERNER: Doesn't that premise that there might be certain social theories about which you could say, as you applied them to particular data, this is definitely and indubitably true?

The question I am really raising is whether there can be that kind of certainty about any theories in their application to social data. In other words, when you criticize these particular theories because they do not give you this feeling of certitude about what you call truth, you are implying that some theories might give you that feeling of certitude. I am challenging that, you see; at least, I am asking whether you can specify any theories that would give you that particular feeling of certitude about any set of social data.

MR. BAIN: It seems to me we will have made a significant contribution to our problem if we can agree that this particular theory does not give us the kind of scientific certitude we are seeking. I understood Mr. Blumer to mean that he questioned the validity of these theories in the same way and for the same reasons that he questions the validity of the instinct theory in interpreting human behavior, viz., that the very terms used in the Thomas-Znaniecki theory, attitudes, values, wishes, etc., are so logically loose and all-inclusive and slippery that the only thing one possibly can get out of it is some kind of literary illumination, as Lerner called it. Therefore, if we can agree that this sort of theory will not do, then we might face the real problem of formulating a theory that would give the kind of certitude you want.

MR. LERNER: I did not say I wanted that certitude.

MR. BAIN: Well, then, the certitude that scientists want.

MR. BLUMER: Mr. Chairman, to keep the record straight, I would like to state that I was not questioning the validity of Mr. Thomas' theories. I was merely stating that one frequently could not determine that validity by the use of the human documents. The theory might be quite valid even though it is not proved by the documentary material.

MR. BAIN: I think you put yourself in an unnecessarily difficult position when you treat a human document as a specific instance of anything. A human document is a reflection of the whole culture in which that human document was produced. It is not the same kind of specific instance with which a chemist is dealing when he mixes sulphuric acid and zinc; it is an entirely different logical concept. In one case, you have the resultant of a whole complicated historical culture reflected or focused in the human document; in the other case, you have a highly abstracted, simplified situation in which the materials have been clearly defined and accurately standardized and the situation itself is one involving variables which are carefully controlled. This is a "specific instance." The human document is nonspecific and largely uncontrolled.

MR. BLUMER: It is specific in the sense one uses it as such. It may not have the admirable features represented by your illustration.

MR. BAIN: There are hundreds of uncontrolled variables in the human documents.

MR. BLUMER: The person using the human document for purpose of definition is using it for a specific set of data out of which he draws his theory or to which he applies his theory; it is specific in that sense. He is conducting a test, presumably.

Mr. Bain: In other words, he is asking the wrong kind of a question.

Mr. Wirth: He isn't so much asking the wrong kind of question; rather, he is seeking to select from the human document those elements which constitute his focus of interest.

Mr. Bain: Yes. To the extent he does that, he is standardizing, or "purifying" the human document and making it a "specific instance" in somewhat the same way that the interaction of "pure" zinc and "pure" sulphuric acid under controlled conditions is a specific instance, though of course, "pure" zinc is an abstraction and the "controlled conditions" are only approximately so.

Mr. Wirth: Yes, but he does that by abstraction. Certainly, Thomas does that by saying this is a case of restlessness or new experience. He says, "Now I am focusing on those elements in the human documents which to me incorporate this particular motive or this particular attitude."

I see no essential difference except that you would have to pare off the complicating factors in the human document by abstraction, whereas, in the chemical case, you would do it by manipulation. This is the great difference between the materials of our discipline and those of other disciplines.

I wonder whether we are not confusing (I am going back to Lerner's first question) two types of what we have called "validity." One is what Max Weber has called "meaningful" validity; the other, "causal" validity. May I be permitted to read a few paragraphs from Weber's[2] discussion of this point?

Gresham's law, as it is called, is, for example, a rationally evident interpretation of human action under specific conditions and under the ideal-typical assumption of purely rational-purposeful action. How far action really corresponds to it, can be demonstrated only by experience

[2] Max Weber, *Wirtschaft und Gesellschaft*, vol. 1, ch. 1

which, in principle, ultimately can be formulated statistically—experience of the factual disappearance of the "good money" from the market; and this experience has really shown that the law has a far-reaching validity. In reality, our knowledge of this phenomenon has developed as follows: the empirical observations came first and then the interpretation was formulated. Without achieving this interpretation, our demand for causal explanation would obviously remain unsatisfied. Without the proof, on the other hand, that the conceptually constructed course of conduct also actually takes place with some frequency, such a "law" though ever so plausible, would be worthless. In this example, there is a thorough agreement between the "meaning adequacy" and the test of experience, and the cases are numerous enough to be regarded as the proof sufficiently certain.

The ingenious hypotheses of Eduard Meyer regarding the causal relevance of the battles of Marathon, Salamis and Palatea, for the peculiar development of Hellenic and subsequently of Occidental culture, is obtainable through a meaningful interpretation of the situation in question and is supported by some "symptomatic" events within this situation (the attitudes of the Hellenic oracles and prophets to the Persians); yet it can be proved only through reference to the examples of what was usually the conduct of the Persians in cases of their victory (Jerusalem, Egypt and Asia Minor), and even then it must necessarily remain imperfect in many respects.

The considerable rational evidence of the hypotheses itself must of necessity provide aid in this difficulty. In very many cases of historical imputation, which appear very plausible, there is lacking however the possibility even of such a proof as was possible in this case. Then, the imputation must definitely remain a "hypothesis."

A "motive" is a meaning-complex, which appears either in the acting individual himself or to the observer as a meaningful reason for his conduct. We apply the term "adequacy of meaning" to a coherent course of conduct when and in so far as, according to our habitual modes of thought and feeling, we recognize the relation of its component parts to be a typical (we usually say "correct") meaning-complex. "Causal adequacy," on the other hand, shall be attributed to a sequence of events when and in so far as there is a chance, according to the rules of experience, that it always may occur in actually the same way. In this sense, for instance, the solution of an arithmetical example which is correct according to our current norms of calculation or thinking is meaningfully-adequate. Within the realm of statistical experience, we will regard as causally adequate the probability of a correct or false solution or of a typical error in calculation or of typical problem-confusion where the probability is arrived at by tested rules of experience, and where the correctness or falsity of the solution is established by our current norms. Hence causal explanation means that according to a rule of probability, estimable in some way, or in a rare ideal case, quantitatively expressed, a certain observed (inner or outer) event will be followed by a certain other event (or will occur in conjunction with it).

I have abbreviated this citation a little bit, but it seems to me that it helps us to differentiate between the insight which enables us to see more meaning in a document than we saw before, and the attempt to arrive at causal explanation, that is, some unvarying general rule.

Mr. Allport: This concept of meaningful validity, I think, has important bearing on our power to predict in the concrete human instance. If prediction is our test of validity, it seems to me, the honors go, not to "causal adequacy," but to "meaningful adequacy" in a given case. For example, I think we can predict what Władek is going to say on important issues in his life, having read the total life and conceptualized it for ourselves, better than we could by a knowledge of all the causal laws of social science or psychology that we may have.

Mr. Wirth: Let us take the case on page 33, where Mr. Blumer speaks of this framework and how you could tell whether a given event not only would be relevant, but whether the framework itself would be relevant to the given event, and, furthermore, whether it would shed any light.

The framework is only a body of definitions, formed according to certain criteria, under which the concrete data are subsumed. The concrete datum in this case is the part of the document which we abstract out of the other parts which are irrelevant. Thus, the fact that John says he does not know what to do with himself becomes, in the Thomas and Znaniecki framework, "restlessness." In this sense, the framework must be sharply distinguished from intimate knowledge of Polish peasant life, which is merely a source for supplementing the partial concrete references in which the letters abound. Both of these are necessary in making a sociological analysis

[121]

of Polish peasant society from letters, but they should not be confused with one another.

Now as to the derivation of this framework, I would certainly agree that it does not matter where it came from, but the task still remains, and I think Mr. Thomas would recognize that, of making more explicit than the Methodological Note does, what the characteristics of this framework are, so that we can correct for the inadequacy of observation or interpretation made according to this framework. The scheme certainly could not be derived from the material itself. To say that it could, is to say that facts speak for themselves. We know facts do not speak for themselves.

Suppose we take the problem of how we can identify or recognize an attitude or value that is asserted to be found in a given document. It seems to me we can recognize it by definition; if the definition is clear-cut and if the description of the concrete data is accurate and adequate with regard to the categories in terms of which attitudes and values are defined, then there should be no difficulty in recognition. But one of the difficulties of recognition is that these concepts, attitude and value, in some measure lack this specificity. I could illustrate this by the concept of value. Now, presumably, the value is something objective; and yet if you try to define the locus of this value, you find that it is subjective. It is the collective subjective which constitutes the value. In other words, the term "objective" in this case is a "weasel" word.

MR. BAIN: So is "the subjective," a weasel word.

MR. WIRTH: Yes, but less so than "the objective" in this case, because "the subjective" becomes a residual concept. Then, let us take the same paragraph (page 34 of Blumer's *Analysis*) where Blumer is worried about how you can determine whether a certain thing corresponds to a certain concept. If the definition is unambiguous and consistently adhered to, both by the analyst and the reader, and if the document under analysis is fairly comprehensive and concrete, it should not be impossible to decide whether the determination is a correct one.

A generalization, by definition, is a proposition bearing on the relationship between certain series of events in most or all cases in which these events are observed. To think that one observation of the coexistence of these events is enough to demonstrate the validity of a generalization is surely a contradiction in terms.

It would be important, therefore, to know, admitting that the insights and hunches of Thomas and Znaniecki are very penetrating, exactly from what they derive their penetration. In other words, we ought to indicate just from what perspective these insights derive their illumination; that might constitute a point of departure for further insight.

I think we all agree that science is invariant relationship, but this cannot be determined from the observation of a single case. The continuous corroboration by inspection of single cases after single cases adds to the security of the generalizations by proving that the relationship as first observed was not the result of factors other than those specified. That is what I think we mean by proof. Single cases can be used (a) to illustrate the plausibility of a hypothesis before it has been tested by a series of observations in a number of cases. They also can be used (b) to illustrate the operation of a relationship already incorporated in a proved generalization. Regarding the security of judgment of the contents of documents, I see no insuperable difficulties if definitions are always unambiguous and exhaustive.

MR. BLUMER: May I ask, Mr. Wirth, can you give any instance of a clear, unambiguous, and exhaustive definition of any social science concept?

MR. WIRTH: No, I have never got one, but I think we have approximations that seem to correspond fairly accurately to our generalizations. Our generalizations can be no more valid than the precision with which our concepts are formulated.

MR. BLUMER: I agree with your statement, but my impression is that in the effort to apply theoretical interpretations to human experience, the more precise and unambiguous the terms become, the less valuable they are.

MR. WIRTH: I agree with that. Take, for instance, the concept of social attitude. Here is a term that is being used in a highly abstract sense and if you pin down those who measure attitudes and ask them what they actually mean by attitude, it comes down essentially to certain verbal utterances made under certain conditions and the classification of those utterances with reference to certain previously established criteria of taxonomy.

MR. BAIN: It comes down to this, the attitude is what this operation measures.

MR. WIRTH: Yes, precisely. But then the question is, are you still dealing with the same sort of thing that Thomas was talking about when he talked about attitudes. I feel that in Thurstone's work, for instance, you are dealing with quite a different thing.

MR. STOUFFER: I wonder about that.

MR. BLUMER: Furthermore, if one took the view of attitude represented by Thurstone's work, or his efforts to define it in terms of operations gone through in a given test, if one took that type of attitude and sought to apply it to the wealth of material in *The Polish Peasant,* you could not make anything out of that material. In other words, that conception of attitude would have been valueless in trying to interpret Polish peasant society as Mr. Thomas has done.

Mr. ALLPORT: Thurstone's operational definition would not have been useful, but his a priori definition would. In terms of what he does with his techniques, it would be utterly valueless, but his simple definition, "Affect for or against objects," could be applied.

Mr. STOUFFER: Yet in at least one study I know of,[3] people using a sophisticated definition of social attitude, when examining a series of case histories, reached almost exactly the same interpretation as to the location of an attitude in terms of its affect, as did some very unsophisticated people who were unfamiliar with *The Polish Peasant* and the literature which followed it.

Furthermore, the judgments derived from analysis of these case histories were almost identical with those obtained by Thurstone's procedure, no matter how you define it. It strikes me that one can ask some very intriguing questions about definitions which may be practically worthless when you come to dealing with the material. Certainly, in the case of social attitudes, I am quite convinced, on the basis of the little work I have done, that the particular definitions one uses in analyzing attitudes with case history material do not make very much difference. In the study referred to, there was a very high correlation between the attitudes obtained by the test procedure and the case history procedure when the cases were analyzed by people who used careful definitions, and by people who used no explicit definitions at all. Now where does that lead us?

Mr. ALLPORT: It means, I think, that the operation did not add anything. The best of sophisticated mathematics

[3] S. A. Stouffer, *An Experimental Comparison of the Statistical and Case Study Method in Attitude Research.* Ph.D. thesis, University of Chicago, 1930

produces about the same result as asking a person just one question, "What is your attitude on the subject?"

MR. STOUFFER: Not necessarily, I think, but your remark could equally well raise the question whether the elaborate operations with the case history procedures are necessary for some purposes. That is, apparently you can get a fairly accurate and valid interpretation of certain simple aspects of behavior by merely asking a question.

MR. WILLEY: Mr. Gallup is doing that right along, isn't he? He does not use any elaborate definitions at all. In fact, he isn't at all certain his questions mean the same thing to all the persons who reply, yet he gets a result that, for his purposes at least, seems to work.

MR. BAIN: He exercises a good deal of care, however, in the formulation of the questions. I noticed a statement the other day that only about 20 per cent of the questions on which he gets responses are finally used because of the sloppiness with which the initial questions were asked.

MR. LERNER: We do not know whether the answers Gallup gets are answers that work. The only time we know it, is when he asks the questions, "Whom are you going to vote for?" Then we know by observing the actual vote whether that particular question worked. When he asks, "What is your attitude toward bringing refugees into this country?" we have no earthly way of knowing whether the result of that question "works." The Gallup experience shows nothing except that when your question is simple enough to be defined in terms of what you are going to do, then the people who give an answer to that proceed to do pretty much what they say they are going to do.

MR. WALLER: I wonder if we might not profitably divide the question? I think we all agree that the methodology worked out by the authors did not in fact describe what they did.

We would like to find out what they did and then pass judgment on that basis. It seems to me we could divide the question into three parts; one, how we find out things; two, how we communicate them after we have found them out; three, how we test our theories or formulations. The way in which we find out things is rather simple. The ability to find out things rests on the ability of the mind to perceive configurations. A concept is a transposable perceptual pattern to which we have given a name. Social theory is a system of concepts which enables us to deal with social reality. Sometimes the concept is quite simple; sometimes it is constructive. Some concepts become highly abstract, e.g., social organization and social rules. Discovery in the social field consists of finding concepts which enable us to perceive social reality.

Now Thomas and Znaniecki brought certain things to their study. They brought a background of preexisting concepts. They brought many fractional and partial concepts and insights, "hunches." This was their apperception mass, perhaps. They also brought logical power. In a recent seminar, the question arose as to whether the great scientist was the least illogical person or the most logical one. I would be inclined to say that he is not merely the least illogical, but also the most constructively logical, logic being defined as the ability to handle concepts in a certain way.

It is obvious, too, that Thomas and Znaniecki had great ability in taking the role of the other, that is, in working out their interpretations largely in terms of projected motives, in imagining what it would be like to be somebody else and to have his will. They also possessed for this job what very few people possess, the ability to fit the scattered pieces of society together in their mind. From this was derived the range and cogency of their theories.

Now their minds worked on this in a certain way, but,

[127]

unfortunately, they had to present their materials in a medium which did not allow them to describe perfectly the way in which their minds worked. They were writing a book; the object of the book was to communicate their insight. In doing this, they were really subject to other imperatives than those of the purely scientific process. The way to communicate insight is to describe phenomena. A perfect example of this is found in Thomas and Znaniecki. They did not describe all the phenomena that passed before their eyes. They described typical phenomena, in part; occasionally, they took phenomena which seemed to be selected at random and showed how their theory worked in explaining that. It is no point against them that they did not present all of their material, because they couldn't. It is not a point against them that possibly some of their interpretations were wrong. That doesn't matter if they adequately communicate a true understanding of something. The compression of presentation is in fact one of the measures of the development of science. Certainly, it is a measure of literary skill.

There arises the question of definition. The definition is simply a set of words which enables people to recognize a perceptual pattern and to identify some subsequently perceived phenomenon as falling into or not falling into that pattern. This, too, they have done very well by their use of all their concrete documents. Very obviously, they could not have done the sort of job that they did without them.

A related question is the degree to which we should present material which allows the reader to differ with us, and differ logically and effectively on the basis of our own materials. This is an imperative that the anthropologists have apparently taken very seriously, more seriously than sociologists have.

The last question, testing the theories, is another we probably all can agree fairly well on: internal coherence, control, which would include prediction and programs of social action, and probably would also include some form of quantification. I think we would have no real difficulty in agreeing on certain tests as at least desirable, nor would we have any doubts, any of us, that very few of our social science materials would pass all of the tests.

MR. WIRTH: Did I understand you to say, Mr. Waller, we could learn something from the anthropologists on this particular question?

MR. WALLER: I do not know whether we can or not. They certainly have done something, haven't they?

MR. WIRTH: Well, I don't know whether they have done it so well. Do they not also argue, for the most part, from single cases? Recently, just to check on this point, I had a student go through some 25 anthropological monographs that have been done in the last twenty years. We found very few instances in which they even took the trouble to delimit the universe on which they were reporting. They left the peripheries almost entirely unbounded. I did it to see how meticulous they are in dealing with this problem of the representativeness of their sampling and I have come to the conclusion on the basis of that investigation that we have very little to learn from them on this point.

MR. NICHOLS: Mr. Blumer, might I ask if you studied at all the practical effect of this study upon the methods of sociology?

MR. BLUMER: No, I haven't made any special study of it, but this work of Thomas and Znaniecki has exerted a tremendous amount of influence among sociologists and has given rise to the rather vigorous prosecution of research involving the use of human documents, especially of life records and life histories. This has become more or less a standard, but not standardized, method in sociological and socio-psychological research.

Further, the theories which they present in the book exercise a great influence on current views of social disorganization and on the theory of community organization. The framework which is sketched there for a social psychology has had, I am sure, a rather wide acceptance. The book has been very influential.

MR. NICHOLS: Has it been useful to social workers in handling immigrant problems and slum conditions?

MR. BLUMER: That I cannot say. Mr. Wirth or Mr. Thomas himself could probably speak about it better than I could.

MR. THOMAS: I do not think it has had much influence on handling the conditions you mention. This movement toward the collection of human document materials was going on inevitably, anyway, that is, in Chicago. So this work was merely another influence on the concrete trend in sociology.

MR. WALLER: Theodore Abel, who is something of a disciple of Znaniecki, seems to think it has affected social work considerably in the handling of immigration.

MR. THOMAS: Well, the whole development of sociology has been reflected in social work, but I do not believe the handling of immigrants has been much affected by this work.

MR. WIRTH: I think I shall have to take issue with that, Mr. Thomas, not that I would be able to put my finger on just what the influence has been with reference to *The Polish Peasant*. It is my belief, however, that the notion of disorganization as a phase of reorganization in a new culture, and the putting of the personality into the context of a social milieu, of a cultural matrix, which is in a state of transition, has had a profound impact upon the mentality of people working in the field of crime. I think it has also had a somewhat negative influence in the sense that the pattern of the four wishes has been more or less slavishly taken over, as such things usually are, so that, like all practical work that follows upon theoretical generalization, it has got them into difficulties. That it has had a great effect upon social work, I think there can be very little doubt.

MR. BAIN: Somewhere in their training, though perhaps not directly from *The Polish Peasant,* most social workers get the idea of the clash of cultures, that the difficulties of immigrants are largely due to the fact that they are disorganized by coming from another culture into this one. It is also true that almost all social workers with whom I have talked in the last ten years speak of the four wishes almost with awe and reverence. And they use them. This is certainly a direct effect of Thomas' work on social workers.

MR. WIRTH: I think it also has helped to rid social workers of their moralistic approach and has helped them to conceive of disorganization, whatever they may mean by that concept, in a more or less naturalistic way. I do not know how much of this is due to *The Polish Peasant* and how much of it is due to other factors.

MR. NICHOLS: Questioning again out of ignorance, has any attempt been made to study other groups in this, or a similar fashion?

MR. WIRTH: I think so.

MR. BAIN: Nothing nearly so intensive.

MR. BLUMER: Nothing so extensive or intensive.

MR. NICHOLS: Has there been an effort to collect similar documents?

MR. WIRTH: Yes.

MR. WALLER: I wonder whether the present concern of the psychoanalysts with anxieties is in any way related to the notion of security as put forward in *The Polish Peasant?*

MR. THOMAS: I don't think there was an appreciable influence in that direction. And there was none in the other direction either. Some sociologists have assumed that I derived the idea of the wish from Freud, but in fact, I was using the term in about the year 1905, and before I had heard of Freud.

With reference to documents, if I may refer back to the question of Mr. Nichols, there is a collection of about 1000 Swedish case studies along the lines of criminology and psychopathology which are, on the whole, superior to anything I have seen. I have also a collection of about 5000 cases which I took from Yiddish publications, mainly from the *Jewish Daily Forward,* which, beginning in 1906, has printed about 15,000.

In Sweden, all the cases in question are kept under observation and studied for a period of from two to six months. They write their stories themselves, but not extensively. They are interrogated at intervals and sometimes by different persons. The authorities communicate with the persons with whom the subjects have associated—relatives, teachers, landlords, employers, neighbors, etc. The replies are very meticulous since the Swedish state can almost command in this respect. I conceive that this material has an all-round superiority to life histories alone.

The Jewish material is limited to the perplexities of a disadvantaged and ritualistic minority group in a new environment, but is practically always a trouble letter and frequently a brief life history beginning with childhood in Europe. The editor purposely developed the life history form of the communication.

I refer only to materials relating to foreigners or the foreign born. It is not necessary to mention the important collection of human documents by the sociologists of the University of Chicago where the practice has been extensive and refined.

MR. BAIN: Then you have changed your idea a little bit about what constitutes "the perfect document"?

MR. THOMAS: I regret a little bit the use of the words "perfect document," but I think the narrative of experience by the individual, whether guided or unguided, is basic, the starting point, in the study of motivation.

MR. BLUMER: Your belief, Mr. Thomas, is that the superiority of this new body of material is due to the fact that it is more exhaustive and detailed? You used the term "superior material."

MR. THOMAS: When we say "superior material," we must ask, "Superior from what standpoint?" The Swedish material has an all-round superiority in the fact that it includes the medical examination, the life history, the controlled interview, the letters to relatives, friends, sweethearts, lawyers, etc., and the testimony of "participant observers." But while this material may be superior in connection with the problems of individuals, it is not necessarily superior for the purpose of tracing cultural processes and changes in a mobile block of a given population. I have referred to this point in my comment on your analysis. But I mentioned only one aspect of the Swedish superiority—the one with which I am most familiar. They have a twenty volume study of Swedish emigration containing, among other things, 289 rather brief life histories, written by Swedish immigrants in America and collected by Lutheran pastors in the northwest. And there are other superiorities which I cannot mention. At the time I worked on *The Polish Peasant,* however, they had not the clinical materials I have described, and at the same time Swedish emigration had practically stopped.

MR. NICHOLS: Mr. Chairman, does the Appraisal Committee intend to put some statement of the practical effects of these studies in the final report? It seems to me this study has had what many theoretical studies have not had—some practical effect. It has had a human value which should be mentioned.

CHAIRMAN THOMPSON: It undoubtedly will appear there, Mr. Nichols.

MR. WIRTH: Apparently you had a preference, when studying the Polish peasant, for spontaneous documents, that is, documents that were actually written in the course of everyday life, rather than documents made to order.

MR. THOMAS: No. The reason for the use of ready-made documents to the extent we did was that they were accessible. We did secure a made-to-order life history which fills one of the original five volumes of our study. The extended life history has an obvious advantage over detached statements in that it reveals the sequences of experience, the total patterning of behavior, motivation, and change. But I will say, from my reading of about 2000 Jewish trouble letters and about 200 of the Swedish documents that masses of letters give some insights which you will miss in autobiographies. The Swedish letters, for example, to and from families, reveal privacies and give insights not found in the autobiographies and institutional interviews.

MR. WIRTH: And the letter has the great value of spontaneity in the sense that it was written in an actual life situation.

MR. THOMAS: Yes.

MR. WIRTH: What is your feeling about the controlled interview?

MR. THOMAS: I value it. The Swedish interviews are a specialized feature, with repetition at intervals, which acts as a control. Shaw's family interview and Hamilton's method in studying marriage are notably good. The psychoanalysts have a very efficient interview technique, if only they did not indoctrinate the subject.

MR. MURDOCK: In estimating the influence of the work, we should consider its effect in adjacent fields, anthropology being one of them. There are at least two types of effect, direct and indirect. Some sociologists have had a direct influence on anthropology, Herbert Spencer, Tarde, Sumner, and so on. I do not perceive a direct influence of this work. I do, however, perceive a significant indirect effect. This work came at a time when sociology was partly philosophical and it introduced a breath of clear air—not only in its scientific approach but in pointing out the importance of human documents and the importance of examining the interrelation between personality and culture. This gave rise, in sociology, to an interest in life history materials which is still increasing. In anthropology, we also see an increasing interest in life history materials. We find more and more workers engaged in getting personal records of various sorts from individual members of primitive society. We see more and more interest in what is called culture and personality. It seems to me that, in large measure, this development in anthropology is an indirect result of this work.

In another adjacent field, we also see an indirect effect. In recent times, there has been an increasing tendency for both psychoanalysts and psychiatrists to become interested in the materials of the social sciences. As long as the social sciences were concerned exclusively with objective materials, there was very little that the psychoanalyst and the psychiatrist could do in conjunction with the social sciences.

Today, I think, we see increasingly the indirect impact of this work, and the work in sociology which it precipitated, in the interest in culture, the integration of culture, and the dynamics of personality in these adjacent fields. In other words, I would say that, outside of the field of sociology, the work under consideration is important, not so much for what it did as for what it started.

MR. BAIN: Do you think that people like Fortune and Mead, and others, were familiar with *The Polish Peasant* as a background for the kind of work they have been doing?

MR. MURDOCK: To what extent they were individually familiar with *The Polish Peasant,* I don't know.

MR. BAIN: Do you think it sort of seeped in?

MR. MURDOCK: It seeped out into anthropological thought, directly and indirectly; perhaps indirectly for the most part.

MR. BAIN: That would be fairly easy to determine. It would be relevant, if we are trying to evaluate the influence of this work on other social sciences. I should think the Committee would like to know that.

MR. LERNER: When we talk of the influence of this work, whether direct or indirect, we are venturing into the history of ideas. This is very worth while, but I think it raises the question of whether that influence has been a good one.

We have been talking about the theories and concepts in the book on several different levels. It is very useful to isolate these concepts, something we have done in social science very considerably. There are literally thousands and thousands of them. Each new social concept both illuminates the subject and obscures it. It illuminates it in the sense that we have a new word to play with, and obscures it in the sense that it adds a further term which must be defined.

I have certain doubts about the utility of definitions as such unless you define from a point of view. Suppose we take the concept of disorganization. We can define it but we haven't gone very far unless we define it in relation to other things. That introduces a new step. If we say, for example, that social or personal disorganization is a step in social or personal reorganization, we have placed that concept in relation to other things. We have related it to other concepts when we attempt to use it. Finally, there is the question of evaluating the extent to which these concepts are either useful or valid. They are valid only in relation to other concepts.

When we are talking about the influence of this book and trying to determine whether that influence has been a good or fruitful one, we have to get away from the fact that it has stated concepts, has added to concepts, or even that its concepts have been employed by others. We have to face the question of whether that employment, such as the way in which the four wishes have been taken up by a large number of people, for example, has been on the whole a beneficial one or a deleterious one. If the discussion could proceed somewhat along these lines, it certainly would be helpful to my thinking.

MR. MURDOCK: Once a concept is set afloat, it undergoes a sort of natural selection; it enters into competition with other concepts. The influences the work has had, particularly the farther you get from the field where it is employed, indicates the success of the concept.

MR. LERNER: It would indicate nothing except the fact that it was being used. For example, a concept might be stated in such a way as to have a high prestige value for sociologists or social workers, let's say, because of its contagious quality. I know that if you were to say "four wishes" to me, my simple mind would say, "Yes, wonderful." You can reduce the personality, or at least the salient elements of it, to four specific things and when I found myself confronting a class in order to appear very impressive, I would say, "Now here are the four wishes." That would indicate nothing about the value of that concept. It would only indicate to my simple mind that the specific enumeration of those wishes had a certain prestige value; it would indicate nothing about the value of the concept. All I am suggesting is that being put in that numerical way may give them a dissemination quality which has nothing to do with their validity.

MR. THOMAS: Mr. Murdock was speaking about the anthropologists who have been getting life histories. Don't you think they are more influenced by psychoanalysis than anything else? For instance, Benedict is definitely influenced by psychoanalysis.

MR. MURDOCK: But until this work showed how these two fields had something to do with one another, it was impossible to get across the border line. I think we ought to point out the importance of the negativistic attitude which the various social sciences have to one another, the relative unwillingness of the anthropologist, let us say, to accept anything from the sociologist. He has to overcome a definite resistance. Whenever we see the anthropologist or the psychoanalyst or the economist taking something that comes from the field of sociology, I think that is one of the criteria that we can advance for the validity of the concept or the subject of study. The anthropologist certainly has not taken over this theoretical system; consciously or unconsciously, he recognizes the strength of the criticism which Mr. Blumer has made. But it has at least indirectly started him to studying types of phenomena which he had not studied before and the validity of the general approach, it seems to me, is suggested by that fact.

MR. POFFENBERGER: I attended a doctors' examination at Columbia in anthropology several days ago. It seems to me the work represented a very close imitation of this study. It was a dissertation on the changes in the Fox Indians, the effect of the clash of that Indian culture with the American culture. Having read *The Polish Peasant* discussion just before, I could see that they seemed to have taken over the technic pretty directly. They did not have written documents. They had verbal material and they attempted to analyze it in just about the same way. In this examination, I raised the question which seems to me to be at the bottom of the work here, how much of what they found there was due to what they took with them into the Fox situation. I asked the candidate how much reading she had done on this question, did she know everything that was known about the Fox Indians before she went there, and if so, how did she protect herself from finding what she was looking for.

Well, the particular candidate said, that due to the press of time, she had not read as much as she would have liked. Then I asked her, suppose she had read everything, how would she have protected herself. She had no answer. I asked what the general anthropological technic was in thus protecting one's self. They certainly would not admit they were entirely ignorant of everything that had been done before. Just as soon as you go in with a certain amount of background, then how do you assure yourself that you are not finding what you knew about before you went there? There is no answer to it at all.

It seems to me, as Mr. Blumer said here in his report, that these findings apparently didn't come directly out of the data which are presented. They certainly came out of those years of contact with the Poles which have been reported here this morning.

MR. MURDOCK: I am glad you pointed out this matter of acculturation because I think that is perhaps another indirect influence in anthropology. Anthropologists today are becoming increasingly more interested in cultural change resulting from the impact of higher civilizations on lower civilizations. This is a recent development in anthropology that has made its appearance since the sociologists have manifested an interest in the changes that result in the assimilation of immigrants, and the like.

MR. WALLER: I should like to point out that one value of the human documents as used by Thomas is that they do correct, in a way, for any preconceptions that the observer has. A life history written without much direction by a naïve person who is not sociologically indoctrinated, giving a view of the world as it seems to him, opens the way to new discoveries for the social scientists and also enables them to make sure that they have a real convergence if the findings of students in other fields fit in with their own.

MR. LERNER: Wouldn't all of us agree on the use of human documents? It seems to me the question is how they are to be used.

MR. WILLEY: That brings me to the point I have been pondering on during this discussion and after reading Blumer's original analysis. He says on pages 27-28:

The methodological approach proposed by Thomas and Znaniecki can and must be viewed on two levels. The first level merely represents the general realization that in social life the influence of cultural and objective factors is dependent on the disposition of individuals and that, consequently, this subjective factor enters into the social life as a vital aspect that cannot be ignored.

I suspect this is the main influence of the book on the other social sciences—that it has emphasized the importance of the subjective factor in making social analyses. Surely that is an important contribution.

Now going on,

The second level of the conception takes the form of presupposing that the relation between the objective and the subjective factors is of the definite sort that is asserted by the methodological formula, and which would give rise, if carried through, to the statement of certain social laws.

I think the significant question is, has the work of Thomas and Znaniecki made it possible for the sociologist or the anthropologist or those in related fields to formulate these social laws? Presumably, that is where the interest of the Committee that brought us together is centered. They are interested in social science research and in the contributions that will further it. I should like to ask Blumer if he thinks the work of Thomas and Znaniecki has made a contribution to the formulation of sociological laws? I know his answer is no, because he says so. Secondly, does he think that this, or any similar approach will lead to the formulation of sociological laws? And, perhaps getting still further away, does he think the formulation of sociological laws corresponding to the laws in the natural sciences is possible?

MR. LERNER: Or desirable.

MR. WILLEY: Desirable, yes. We end on a facetious note. Lerner can correct me, as his memory is probably better. Gertrude Stein said she had an infallible test for a genius. Whenever she met one, a little bell rang inside her. I am wondering, if in evaluating such theoretical frameworks as the one now under discussion, we are saying more than is valid because "a little bell rings inside of us."

My purpose in injecting myself into the discussion is to shift it, if possible, to this second question of the possible contribution to research of the type of analysis that Thomas and Znaniecki have so admirably carried forward.

MR. BLUMER: I am quite clear they have not established any social laws. They propose a few, make tentative attempts at others, but quite clearly they have not established any.

In answer to your second question, I personally don't think, that with their formulation, it would be possible to arrive at social laws because of the fundamental ambiguity that surrounds their concepts of attitude and value which they presuppose as being capable of having distinct temporal distinction, and consequently, of being separate from one another, and therefore capable of leading to a rather specific causal relation. My own view is that this is not true, and, consequently, since you are just asking for my judgment, I do not believe that with their formulation it would be possible to arrive at social laws.

With respect to your third question, as to whether it is possible to get social laws in social science, I have to answer by saying I don't know. I am rather skeptical.

MR. WILLEY: That is a rather vital point, though, isn't it, even going back to the Methodological Note? Because the assumption there is that one is going through all of these analyses looking toward the ultimate objective of control.

MR. BLUMER: That is true. I think, however, that while the negative applies to these questions, the fact remains that *The Polish Peasant* may be exceedingly valuable as a contribution to social research.

MR. LERNER: Research for laws or research for something else?

MR. WILLEY: On which of the two levels you specify on pages 27-28?

MR. BLUMER: On the first, because I am ruling out the second. Research could be very fruitful from the standpoint of giving us understanding—intelligent, and fundamental, or at least, better, comprehension of the behavior. It may even result in better efforts at control even though the new knowledge cannot be reduced to the precise cause and effect relationships which we regard as necessary for science.

MR. BAIN: That is, you think social research must lie somewhere between what we ordinarily think of as scientific laws, as one pole, and another, which we perhaps can call literary insight, or illumination? That social research is a kind of legitimate research that isn't quite scientific and yet isn't quite damned by being purely literary?

MR. BLUMER: Well, I would even accept your formulation, and I also think that is what we have in the social sciences.

MR. BAIN: Do you also think we have to remain in this predicament?

MR. BLUMER: Well, in terms of the present situation, that would be my supposition. One can only derive one's inference from what the present situation is. You can project a hope that it will be different sometime in the future. I likewise project that hope.

MR. STOUFFER: Would you extend your skepticism to the so-called laws of economics—for example, Engel's laws? It would seem that there has been fairly good agreement among economists on Engel's laws. They may be modified; the recent Consumer Purchases study, for example, may lead to some modifications. Still, there is a number of generalizations which might be given the character of laws, i.e., generalizations which are true to a high degree of probability.

MR. BAIN: Which is all you have in the "laws" of the physical and biological sciences.

MR. STOUFFER: If such generalizations are possible in economics, why not in sociology?

MR. BLUMER: I wouldn't want to speak for the economists; it is not my field. I have the impression that there is an enormous amount of controversy and disagreement among them as to these presumed laws, particularly those that were supposedly set up by the classical economists.

MR. STOUFFER: The question is whether or not we must take a nihilist attitude toward possibilities of scientific laws in sociology. It seems to me that we have sufficient agreement on at least a few generalizations in economics to suggest the possibility of laws in other fields of social science as well.

MR. LERNER: You get a nihilist attitude if you set up a goal which is inherently unattainable, but if you set up a less ambitious goal, one that doesn't even claim that high degree of probability you get in the physical sciences—and I agree it is only a high degree of probability—you will escape nihilism, which is merely the disillusionment that comes when we are not able to achieve what we had hoped to achieve. I question the whole comparison that I have found so often being made between the natural sciences and social sciences. I think one of the things we have suffered from has been that sense of inferiority that comes from our not being able to turn ourselves into natural scientists. I think we ought to recognize that and also recognize that there are attainable social generalizations that are worth making, and then to talk about research in terms of getting at those relatively attainable generalizations.

MR. ALLPORT: Would it be an implication of Mr. Blumer's position, since he is optimistic about the first level and not the second, that psychological laws are more easily found than sociological laws?

MR. NICHOLS: Have you any in mind?

MR. ALLPORT: I thought it followed because he says the recognition of the subjective factor in social life is perhaps the major source of influence of the work here under discussion. He draws attention to that and seems optimistic about the further study of this subjective factor. Would that not imply the possibility of finding psychological generalizations before we get to the level of sociological generalization?

MR. BLUMER: No, I wouldn't think that. Of course, one is thrown back here, I suppose, to the definition of the terms psychological and sociological. If one remains inside the framework which Thomas and Znaniecki have proposed, of reducing social life abstractly to interaction between attitudes and values, then presumably that would lend itself to the formulation of generalizations, either with respect to the factor of value or with respect to the factor of attitude.

MR. ALLPORT: Yes, that is my point. Aren't we apt to get farther on the study of attitude than we are with the study of interaction of attitudes and values?

MR. BLUMER: I doubt it. I question the possibility of studying attitudes without taking into consideration their values.

MR. WILLEY: Isn't there an intermediate field between the two levels here—one, the mere recognition of the fact that there is the cultural influence on the individual, and second, the formulation of laws? Isn't there an intermediate field in which you may not have research that gives you the exactness that you envisage in a scientific law in a natural field, but none the less gives you generalizations which, even for practical purposes of control, are very good, and that the problem of the social scientist, the sociologist at least, is the development of these generalizations which are not exact laws but which none the less may be useful, even in matters of control?

MR. LERNER: We go beyond the mere statement that there is a relationship.

MR. WILLEY: It seems to me that there is a second step there which Blumer has left out and to which Thomas and Znaniecki have made an enormous contribution.

MR. BLUMER: I don't regard it as a second step. That is what I mean by the first level. Thomas and Znaniecki have produced a wealth of theoretical generalizations, some of which are exceedingly valuable and penetrating; but they are not stated in the form of laws.

MR. WILLEY: It seems to me that your present statement rather restricts the meaning of the first level as given in your

Analysis. The subjective factor enters into social life and its final aspect may not be ignored. They have made that contribution, but haven't they gone further and made certain generalizations with respect to social life that are not laws?

MR. BLUMER: Lots of them; yes, certainly. That is what we are dealing with and it is those that I have sought to consider in their relation to the materials.

MR. LERNER: You say they are valuable, but you can't tell how valuable they are.

MR. BLUMER: Yes. This involves the question of judgment, which so far has been ignored in this discussion. Let's say you read the theoretical statements of Thomas and Znaniecki and the materials to which the authors specifically relate these theoretical remarks. You then make the judgment as to how reasonable it is. If it seems to be a reasonable interpretation, you accept it. That raises the question, what is a reasonable interpretation? Well, it seems to me that there is a kind of triadic relationship there. A reasonable interpretation is largely dependent upon the ability of the person who makes the generalization. I should expect a person like Mr. Thomas who has had much intimate contact with human beings, who has studied them extensively, who has marked ability in understanding human nature, on the whole to make a reasonable interpretation. Furthermore, there is a body of material there; you can read that. It is human material; you can assume the role of the person whose account it is and thus arrive at some idea of how reasonable the interpretation is.

Then, too, you bring your own background of experience. If you are a person who has had a lot of contact with human beings and understands human nature well, and particularly, if you already have a knowledge of the particular people with which the authors are dealing, you are in a better position to judge the reasonableness of the interpretation. Thus, the judgment of the reasonableness of an interpretation is based upon the background of the reader's own experience and also upon the authority of the person who makes the interpretation.

MR. MURDOCK: Doesn't that presuppose you will have a plurality of interpretations?

MR. BLUMER: That is what happens.

MR. MURDOCK: You cover a body of material with several alternative interpretations and the reasonable interpretation is the one that fits best.

MR. WIRTH: It seems to me that Thomas and Znaniecki have gone farther than that. I would like to raise the question whether there is not to be found a marginal field of scholarly, if not scientific, endeavor lying between the meaningful description of the unique and the formulation of invariant universal laws. In what sense is the middle point of that continuum qualified? Is it culturally circumscribed? That is, can you make your generalization only for the Polish peasant group? Is it temporally qualified, or is it qualified by some other condition of time, space, or circumstance? Would you concede that generalizations are possible within such a relatively limited universe?

MR. BLUMER: Yes.

MR. WIRTH: If that is so, couldn't there be, possibly, an objective test of the validity of some of these theories? For instance, suppose I read into Thomas and Znaniecki's *Polish Peasant* the general proposition, Given a culture, that is, a set of social values, in which a given population lives, then if that population is transferred to a society which has a different set of values, the old values can persist for a certain period of time. It seems to me that could be tested, we will say, in the case of the Polish peasant's attitude toward land. Mr. Thomas pointed that out. He pointed out that the Polish peasant tends

[147]

to acquire land in America. This is not statistically proved, but it is statistically provable, it seems to me. The Polish peasant tends to buy a house and lot more readily than an immigrant from some other society. Here is a possible objective test of the validity of a theoretic interpretation. Why couldn't you devise other objective tests of the validity of some of these theories?

MR. BLUMER: I quite agree with you. There is no reason why such simple assertions as the example you give should not be tested by accounts of experience, but as one moves from that to a more abstract theoretical conception such as the way attitudes are undermined when individuals acquire an increased desire for new experience, the ease with which one can use that documentary material for purposes of testing becomes less and less.

MR. WIRTH: If we are going to end on this note of utter nihilism, it comes down to the prestige or force of the assertor as to whether a given proposition is valid or not. If that isn't the case, then we obviously must look for certain other criteria of validity, be they universal, partially universal, or relatively unique. I don't know whether the law of marginal utility, or Engel's law, holds for all cultures, but there is apparently some objective evidence which no sensible person will dispute, that these generalizations are at least approximately correct, not merely plausible. In other words, we can act as if they were correct and thus increase the effectiveness of our action.

So, if I were to formulate a sociological law, e.g., that institutions continue to exist for other reasons than those that got them started, it might be a useful generalization. If Thomas states that whenever an individual transplants himself from one culture to another, he experiences these stresses and strains indicated by the terms disorganization and reorganization, the generalization has an actual value in the observation of new data and in the understanding of behavior in certain instances. Thomas and Znaniecki may not have exhausted the universe with which they were dealing but they at least have formulated hypotheses to be tested by their own or other evidence.

MR. BLUMER: I think Gresham's and Engel's law, and many similar ones, are more or less on the objective level of values; one is merely seeking to relate value to value, which can be done. It is only when one attempts to state a proposition which involves the interaction of values and attitudes that I question whether we have any laws in sociology comparable to Engel's. Thomas's and Znaniecki's avowed intention, of course, was to find such laws in this field of subjective and objective (attitude and value) behavior.

A moment ago, I was maneuvered by Mr. Willey into the expression of my personal opinion. I am skeptical of our being able to develop any very exact laws which involve this factor of subjective human experience, but I do not see anything nihilistic in this position because it is possible to develop a body of very useful knowledge in the form of generalizations even though they are not exact, or invariant, enough to be called laws. Further, one can formulate two or three competing propositions applicable to the same given field and make some distinction between them in terms of how suitable they are.

This is a matter of judgment, but it isn't wholly an arbitrary matter, because I distinctly feel that one who has an intimate familiarity with the people and the type of experience with which he is dealing will make propositions which will seem more reasonable than would be true of propositions proposed by someone who lacks such knowledge. I don't see that I am led into a nihilistic or pessimistic position because I rely upon my judgment of the reasonableness of such propositions. We can differentiate between judgments; some are better and some are poorer.

MR. WILLEY: There is the rub, isn't it, how you determine whether the judgment is good or bad, better or poorer?

MR. LERNER: Not only the rub, it is the fundamental question I had in mind. We recognize that one judgment is better than another. The question is, how do we know that?

CHAIRMAN THOMPSON: Suppose we leave that question for this afternoon and go to lunch now.

AFTERNOON SESSION

CHAIRMAN THOMPSON: I think we should start. We stopped at a definite question. Mr. Lerner, would you repeat your question?

MR. COKER: The question was, How do we know one judgment is better than another?

MR. LERNER: I believe we are on extremely dangerous speculative ground when we judge a proposition to be sound, or reasonable, because of the prestige or the authority of the person making it—because he has had considerable contact with human beings and, therefore, ought to know. If you proceed along those lines, you are getting into the realm where people may impose their authority, first, through rational persuasion; second, through irrational persuasion; and finally, through force.

MR. BLUMER: What I remarked was that the investigator could make a more reasonable interpretation if he had some gift for understanding human beings, and if, in addition, he had some familiarity with the kind of experience that he was studying, than a person lacking this knowledge; and that the latter, therefore, naturally would be disposed to extend some deference to the superior competence of the investigator. The

[150]

implication you have drawn from this remark, viz., that we must become slaves to authority, is not the one I would draw. Rather, I would say that one competent to judge whether an author has made a reasonable interpretation must be an expert in the field, i.e., one who has both the ability to understand human beings and also an extensive familiarity with the materials being studied. Now one who does not possess these two traits should defer to the judgment, or prestige, if you prefer, of the investigator. I do not see that such deference to expert knowledge, or judgment, carries with it any such pessimistic implication as the one you have just drawn.

Mr. LERNER: I would say that you don't accept a man's judgment because he is an expert. You count him as expert because you have evaluated his judgment and found it adequate. That is, I would reverse the whole process.

Mr. BLUMER: Yes, but when the authors of *The Polish Peasant* apply a series of interpretations to a series of documents, you find that you cannot answer the question, Does the document bear out this interpretation? You can only say, "Well, the interpretation seems to be very reasonable." Then one is thrown back to the question of the competence of the authors. If one knows something about them, their experience and other works, and if one also knows *The Polish Peasant*, one must admit that they have an extensive subjective and objective familiarity, not only with Polish peasants, but also with our own culture. One would, therefore, be disposed to say, "Yes, this interpretation, while not definitely tested by the documenting material, is probably a very good one."

Mr. LERNER: That is what I would question. I would have a predisposition to respect a man's conclusions or interpretations because of his past experience, but it would be only a predisposition, and I would still have the problem before me as to whether that particular interpretation might be erroneous, while another might be all right.

MR. BLUMER: How are you going to answer that? How are you going to handle that problem?

MR. LERNER: That is the real question. What are the tests of what you call the reasonableness of the interpretation? The knowledge that a man has had a wide contact with human beings and is very familiar with a particular field is far from being a conclusive test that his interpretations are sound; in fact, it is just the beginning of such a test in the sense that you are now willing to listen to him. You still have the entire problem of making the test.

MR. BLUMER: I should agree with you. Recognizing that one can distinguish between judgments in terms of their reasonableness, the question arises, On what basis does one make that distinction?

MR. WALLER: Frequently, we judge an interpretation to be reasonable, I think, when it organizes and makes intelligible to us what we already know. Many great advances in the social sciences have come, not from new discoveries, but from organizing conceptions which made old discoveries intelligible. Much was known about those scattered phenomena of conscious and unconscious mental conflict, before Freud came along and gave us a theory. Similarly, with the class struggle hypothesis; similarly, with the concept of folkways and mores. After a person has given you a number of conceptions which have made your own experience more intelligible, you tend, perhaps, to follow him to the next step and so to believe something that may not be true.

MR. LERNER: The problem isn't why the class struggle hypothesis has had as much spread as it has. The real problem is, to what extent is the class struggle hypothesis valuable, or valid? Suppose you have two antithetical theories which organize experience for large groups of people. Should the test be the degree of acceptance, the size of the following? If so, you have the temptation of widening the following for an idea by irrational rather than rational appeals. We see this going on in several cultures today. Ultimately, I think, it results in the appeal to authority and force. Certainly the test of the validity of the Aryan race hypothesis is not the fact that the German people seem to be agreeing on it.

MR. WALLER: I think, to a degree, diffusion—at least, in our scientific universe—does tend to be somewhat proportional to the validity or importance attributed to scientific work.

MR. WIRTH: It seems to me there are a few canons of judgment that we generally follow in such instances. A valid theory has to have a certain amount of logical consistency, which may be nothing more than mere plausibility; and it must not violate any canon of logical thinking. A second canon certainly would be that the theory must not violate that body of knowledge, more general than the theory in question, which we have already taken for granted, either from other disciplines, or from experiences that seem to be fairly well founded. A third canon, is that we should examine a hypothesis in the light of alternative hypotheses. We accept that hypothesis, other things being equal, which explains the most with the least assumptions.

There are also certain other canons, e.g., we assume there is some objective reality corresponding to our subjective experience, or at least symbolized by it. So, when we look for corroborative testimony, we sometimes take this objective reality which no one would dispute and use it to test our theory. We may say, e.g., that the number of people of one kind in jail is arbitrary, but, upon investigation, it also may be discovered that imprisonment is related to the experiences the prisoners have had with their particular customs or traditions or norms. All of these things put together, and doubtless many more, give us more than a mere snap judgment, or mere personal prejudice, about the validity or nonvalidity of a given theory.

MR. BAIN: If one is faced with a problem such as Blumer was describing, he ordinarily tries to rephrase the question so it can be tested empirically. If this cannot be done, it is either the wrong kind of question, or one that will have to wait, so far as a scientific answer is concerned.

MR. WIRTH: Yes, but I would say one way to begin the analysis of a given theory is to inquire into the particular perspective which prompted this particular author to arrive at these particular conclusions or hypotheses. Having discovered that, i.e., what he took for granted, I would say, "Now suppose we take something else for granted, at what conclusions would we arrive?"

MR. BLUMER: What would that lead to?

MR. WIRTH: It might result in two opposing theories. Then I would ask, which one requires the most assumptions, and which one is more consistent with what we already know?

MR. BAIN: Would either, or any, of the analytic methods you are discussing eventually lead you to a point where you would have to formulate a hypothesis capable of being tested by the empirical methods commonly used in the various sciences?

MR. WIRTH: Yes. We haven't really discussed this enough. We ought to realize that any proposition is valid only within a certain system, within a certain set of postulates with which we begin, and over a certain area of reference to which the data have relevance.

Having decided that, I would then try to exhaust, as completely as possible, that particular universe. I wouldn't immediately arrive at a law—I would have just a hypothesis—until I couldn't find any more cases that I couldn't fit into my theory. Thus, in time, my theory might become a law. This is the way all people who want to get fairly valid knowledge must proceed.

MR. BLUMER: Do you know of instances of this in the social sciences? Do you think you could ascertain the basic assumptions of the many conflicting social science theories and find out which had the fewest, and finally accept it as the best theory, and rule out all others?

MR. WIRTH: I think I could do it in some limited field if I could define my field strictly enough. I think your own analysis of the failure of the instinct hypothesis this morning is a good example.

MR. LERNER: Isn't Blumer really asking for an instance of a hypothesis that will stand up—not one that can be punctured?

MR. WIRTH: Well, I think in this case you have a hypothesis that will stand up, namely, the contrary hypothesis to the instinct hypothesis.

MR. LERNER: There are no social instincts?

MR. WIRTH: No. I would even state it more positively. People tend to excel in those things in which they have had a cumulative tradition, that is, the thing has been singled out as a matter of importance and interest to them, they have been trained along those lines, it has been held up to them as something worth while. Everything being equal, people will do those things rather than the things we attribute to their germ plasm.

MR. LERNER: The historical conditioning of national character?

MR. WIRTH: Yes; in a general way, the cultural conditioning theory would take the place of the instinct hypothesis.

MR. LERNER: It seems to me you are dealing now with a field of inquiry rather than with a theory, or at least with a theory on what Blumer called the first plane, i.e., the mere statement that there is some relationship between factors. When, however, we deal with theories like the class struggle, or the instinct of aggression, or Freudianism, we are dealing with a particular formulation of that relationship, which, I take it, was what Blumer was asking—Can you give a formulation of such a relationship which stands up under the test that you have applied?

MR. WIRTH: I don't think I was merely denoting a field of inquiry. I was actually stating a positive proposition that adequately explains a given phenomenon in cultural life. If you call that a field of inquiry, well, then I don't know what a proposition is.

MR. LERNER: But how useful is a proposition which has so indefinite an extension? Shouldn't we go beyond such a statement?

MR. WIRTH: You might want to look for a great many subsidiary propositions that have more specificity. Is that it? I think that is quite possible. I think many such have been formulated.

MR. LERNER: It would help a great deal if we would really examine one. So far we have not concentrated on any specific theory to see how it works out.

MR. BAIN: That is, you want to discuss something in connection with this general theory of cultural conditioning which would be as specific, say, as the evolution of the muskrat is, in relation to the general theory of organic evolution?

MR. LERNER: The class struggle is an extremely good one to analyze. I will confess I have no way of convincing myself of its validity. I have read a lot that other people have said about it and I still find no way of evaluating their opinions.

I do evaluate it, for myself, of course, but you may not recognize the validity of my evaluation, unless, as Blumer suggests, you think I have a good deal of experience with these things, and, therefore, have a certain amount of plausibility in what I say.

Try to evaluate the validity of the class struggle theory. It is very specific, namely, that the succession of institutions and social organization in every culture is determined by the struggle between the class which controls the means of production and the other classes which are in dependence upon the first class; and that all systems of cultural organization, idea systems, and other social phenomena, emerge out of this struggle. Or take any other theory.

Mr. Wirth: The difficulty with this particular theory is that the concepts you use, class, class struggle, means of production, and so forth, always have been highly ambiguous concepts, and still are. When you begin to define them, then either that proposition or theory gets to be meaningless, or if it does mean something, you restrict investigation to a much narrower field of inquiry.

In fact, there is much controversy about this matter, e.g., in his study of Calvinism and capitalism, Max Weber tried to put it the other way round. It seems to me that social scientists should clarify the terms of their propositions, rather than go ahead at random trying to find out whether a highly ambiguous proposition is true or not. We are just now beginning to analyze the concept class. Until fifteen or twenty years ago, we just took it for granted.

Mr. Bain: The length of time you discuss a question has no significance if you have asked the wrong kind of question to begin with. The scientists in the various fields who have got on with their work are those who have highly developed the art of asking the right kind of questions, i.e., questions that are susceptible of empirical testing. For more than 2000 years, men discussed the attributes of God, but we haven't much more light on that question now than we had 2000 years ago, because it is the kind of a question that a natural scientist would never ask. Social scientists are still asking many questions that other natural scientists would laugh at. We are long on words, usually undefined or ill-defined, and very short on scientific results.

MR. ALLPORT: Kornhauser attempted to find out whether there were any common attitudes that characterized economic classes as such. He found a few that did, within certain probabilities, and a good many that didn't. I happen to remember one that didn't. To the question, Do you want a better opportunity for your children than you had?, 100 per cent said "Yes," absolutely regardless of class difference. That is, we cannot comprehend the variables that enter into class consciousness until we get way below the nonspecific level of the class struggle and get down to such problems as frustration and attitudes and the very difficult problem of pattern, until ultimately we come down to case study again.

It seems to me, Mr. Wirth gave first an extremely broad generalization and many of us seem to agree that it hasn't much value. The class struggle is also a generalization that seems to me does not get beyond the verbal stage because it is not yet reduced to specific hypotheses. When you do reduce it to specific hypotheses capable of being tested by specific empirical methods, I think you will find you are investigating problems relating to the attitudes of the single individual.

MR. LERNER: What are the criteria for knowing that we are making progress in the validation of this particular hypothesis? Isn't it possible that Marx gave a sharper formulation of the class struggle theory than modern writers have done?

[158]

MR. WIRTH: We have made progress in formulating the criteria of class, in learning how ambiguous the term was in the early Marxist writing and how many variables it contained. This seems like progress to me.

MR. BLUMER: Have we made the term clear?

MR. WIRTH: No, but we have made it clearer than it was. We know a little more about the numerous factors that are involved; we know that when people talked about class, they frequently were talking about different things. We know that such a cosmic theory as that of class struggle is certainly not very specific. Like many other cosmic theories, the class struggle theory has become a fighting weapon and a cult. It has been a question of who could shout the loudest, not who could present the most convincing evidence. In the social sciences, we have largely failed to put our theories to the test of rigorous logical analysis and cumulative empirical investigation as has been done in the physical and biological sciences. We have made some progress, certainly, in recognizing that we don't know.

MR. LERNER: I wonder whether that is the only kind of progress we can make?

MR. WIRTH: Well, we might call it positive progress when you find most writers agreeing that if you define class in a certain way, then within certain limits, some of these propositions can be proved by the limited historical materials which are relevant. We also agree that if you define it differently, you arrive at different conclusions. We also have found that there is much more to the problem than this assumed one-sided relationship between the technological substructure and the attitudinal superstructure. We think there is more reciprocal interaction between them.

MR. LERNER: Engels started with the mutuality of relationship.

MR. WIRTH: It was forgotten when the class struggle theory became a cult.

MR. LERNER: That is very often what happens. You start with clarity and the thing becomes obscured as you attempt to act upon it; it becomes further obscured when you break up what seems to be a single concept into what seems to be its components. Then somebody discovers that the original statement was better than later ones.

MR. ALLPORT: We can test Marx scientifically if we want to. We can define class provisionally and then study all the traits the members of an alleged class ought to have. Probably we shall find that we have a continuum instead of a bimodal distribution, and that we have to limit our concept of class to certain combinations of traits, or attitudes. Then we can find out whether people with these trait-combinations really do quarrel with each other—whether they carry out the struggle Marx claimed. In this way, we can test these grand generalizations, or some of them, empirically. If we find the "grand myths" are wrong as stated, we probably shall find also that they can be reinterpreted, that is, there may be a residuum of truth in Marx which will explain why people with certain attitudes and opinions and frustrations will quarrel with one another.

MR. BAIN: Those grand generalizations always get tested by being broken up into a great number of simple problems. What we call "progress" in all the natural sciences, among which I would include the social sciences, has come about through the development of the art of stating simple and unequivocal propositions, or hypotheses, which are capable of empirical test. When enough such propositions have been tested and retested and all of them are logically consistent with the grand generalization, it may be said to be verified. The empirical verification of no one single hypothesis relevant to the general theory of organic evolution can be said to be adequate proof of it, but when thousands of such simple single hypotheses have been verified, and they all hang together—none of them are clearly verified negative cases—we eventually come to accept the general theory of organic evolution as an actual valid scientific fact. Many similar examples could be given from the history of the physical and biological sciences.

In the social sciences, more so in some others than in sociology, perhaps—though it certainly is still largely true in sociology—the procedure has been just the opposite. We refuse, or lack the scientific imagination, ability, or morale, to define our problems with a sufficiently small number of controlled variables so that a definite, clear-cut, unequivocal, empirical test of our hypotheses can be made. That is what is the matter, I think, with ninety years of verbal to-do over Marxism. As Wirth says, there has been much shouting but little logical analysis and empirical investigation. If thousands of small problems relevant to the general class struggle theory had been formulated so as to be capable of empirical test, and if they had been tested, one after the other, with thousands and thousands of man-hours of intensive research, there should have emerged either a refutation or a confirmation of the general class struggle theory.

In the case of evolution, literally millions of man-hours have gone into the testing of thousands of small, clearly defined, few-variable propositions, until finally there has emerged such an enormous body of logically consistent and empirically derived knowledge relevant to the general theory of organic evolution that we accept it as a verified scientific fact. The same thing is true of all the more inclusive theories in the biological and physical sciences. Scientists in these fields have always proceeded by making small specific hypotheses that seem relevant to the general theory—hypotheses capable of being tested and retested by any competent man. If the results all hang together, if there is cumulative confirmation, the inclusive generalization becomes a verified scientific principle. This is the only procedure, I am sure, by which the social sciences can escape from the dark morass of bewildering words in which they flounder.

Mr. Blumer: What you say sounds plausible, but I question whether this reduction to simple situations in sociology, at least, does not really mean the loss of the original problem. I notice that when vague and indefinite concepts are broken down into very precise and definite terms that can be tested empirically, it frequently happens that those simple terms cannot be recombined to produce the original concept.

Mr. Bain: Which raises the question as to whether the original concept was anything more than a nice ear-filling combination of scientifically meaningless words.

Mr. Blumer: That is possible, but when you try to apply these simple empirically tested terms to the type of situation to which the original concept referred, you very frequently find that there is no application at all. In short, there was some intrinsic part of the situation to which the original concept referred, however vaguely and imprecisely, to which you can no longer refer at all when the original concept has been reduced to these simple terms. The original thing is lost.

Mr. Bain: Such a situation raises the question of the validity of the original theory; it tends to make explicit the implicit postulates with which you started.

Mr. Waller: It also raises the question of the validity of breaking the thing down into atoms. It is true that Beard's economic determinism, economic interpretation of history, is vastly better documented, vastly more accurate, than the original Marxian theory.

MR. LERNER: It is better documented, and also it is far more simple than Marx. Beard's economic interpretation of the constitution is based upon a conception of class in terms of direct economic pressure upon individuals because they happen to own stocks and bonds and notes, and so on.

This is a good illustration of the tendency to vulgarize and simplify a concept from its original formulation and then apply to the vulgarized and simplified concept, the entire elaborate apparatus of technical research—looking through documents and going through Treasury Department manuscripts, and so on. In other words, Beard attempted a *tour de force*, but I think Marx's original formulation of the concept of class was vastly superior to Beard's, because class, in Marxian terms, does not depend upon the direct impact of personal economic interest; it depends upon the indirect impact of economic interests, as they come through the ideology of the entire culture, upon persons that are tied to that ideology.

MR. BAIN: When you introduce "indirect influences," you destroy any possibility of an empirical scientific verification.

MR. LERNER: If that is so, we ought to shift our base and not expect a scientific verification in your sense.

MR. ALLPORT: Don't you think, Mr. Lerner, that you can test your hypothesis that influences originate in an ideology of a culture through the study of symbols and their specific effects upon individuals?

MR. LERNER: I have certain ideas about the validity of the class struggle hypothesis, but I can't verify it from documents found in the Treasury Department because they deal with elements in the life history of individuals, with elements in their intellectual processes, and so on, that I can't get at. If I could get at them, I still couldn't verify the class struggle theory by any one set of data.

Mr. Wirth: Wouldn't you agree that meticulous study of hundreds of highly abstract, segmentalized, but relevant aspects of the class struggle theory might ultimately enable you to extract all that is investigable about this theory?

Mr. Lerner: I wish I could accept this notion of scientific progress—I would like to. We all recognize that just as many man-hours are being put into the social sciences as the natural sciences but they don't clarify because they are not being directed properly, or because—and I think this is the case—you can't break up a problem of this kind in the social sciences in the way you could break it up in the natural sciences.

Mr. Bain: We have never tried it, certainly. Largely because of the prevalence of the view you have just expressed, the man-hours of research in the social sciences are directed toward seeking to answer the wrong kinds of questions, i.e., questions that cannot be answered by rigorous, empirical research. We still like large, loose, diffuse, all-inclusive questions like the validity of the class struggle theory. We like questions that leave plenty of scope for the imagination and do not require much work, except the writing of millions of words that no one can understand very clearly. We are still in the shouting stage.

Mr. Allport: I think we have tried, to a certain extent, but we haven't yet synthesized our results. I can name half a dozen specific, limited studies on the class struggle—Cantril, Hartman, Kornhauser, and Stagner—studies that bear on attitudes toward Fascism in relation to income, on class appeals and their effect on attitudes. There are several such studies. The trouble is, nobody has synthesized them. If somebody would do this, we might revise our concept of Marxism. It isn't a question of whether it is true or false, but how far is it true, in what sense is it true.

Mr. Bain: The present organic evolutionary theory is the

result of the cumulative scientific knowledge derived from millions of man-hours devoted to specific, well defined, few-variable hypotheses capable of empirical testing, but the theory as formulated by Darwin has been superseded—practically all of it.

MR. LERNER: Haven't we replaced it by another theory of evolution?

MR. BAIN: No, Darwin's general theory that organisms change, that species are mutable, still stands. It has been verified by seventy-five years of intensive investigation, but not by the methods nor the ideas of Darwin. These have been superseded in almost every case, or at least play a very different role in modern evolutionary theory than they did in Darwin's day. A great many things, scientific facts and mechanisms relevant to organic evolution of which Darwin knew nothing, have been found out.

MR. LERNER: We are agreed that social systems change but the theory of the class struggle purports to furnish a dynamic of that change. We are not agreed on the dynamic.

MR. BAIN: Darwin furnished a theoretic dynamic for biologic change but it didn't stand up.

MR. LERNER: Do the natural sciences know what the dynamic of change in life is?

MR. BAIN: We know a number of things Darwin didn't know, and one of the reasons is because he proposed a system of dynamics to account for the changes that were observed. His theories were tested and new knowledge was obtained which compelled us to revise most all of his theoretical interpretations. These millions of man-hours of intensive research on carefully delimited problems eventually produced a body of verified scientific knowledge which has been synthesized into the general system of evolutionary theory we have today. It is almost certain that both the data and the general theory, since they are reciprocally related, will be somewhat different tomorrow, but in the meantime we have a fairly coherent theoretical formulation within which and by which we can do further intensive specific research and thereby learn more about the dynamics of biological change.

MR. WIRTH: Mr. Chairman, would you permit me to read a paragraph into the record? I have the permission of the author. Mr. Thomas wrote this in 1928 in reply to a question Mr. Park asked about his method of studying the Polish peasant. He said, among other things, the following:

It is my experience that formal methodological studies are relatively unprofitable. They have tended to represent the standpoint developed in philosophy and the history of philosophy. It is my impression that progress in method is made from point to point by setting up objectives, employing certain techniques, then resetting the problems with the introduction of still other objectives and the modification of techniques. For example, Galvani or someone else gets a reaction from a frog's leg by the application of electricity. This may suggest to Pfeffer or Verworn the application of electricity to a basin containing infusoria. It is then determined that these organisms show positive and negative reactions, that these reactions are dependent upon the state of nutrition, etc., and the whole question of the tropisms is opened up. These and other investigators then introduce other stimuli—heat, light, acids, food, hard surfaces, etc.—and get still other reactions. There is then developed a mechanistic school of behavior and Loeb devotes himself, among other things, to the attempt to secure by certain manipulations reactions from inorganic material identical with those shown by living material. At this point Jennings, conditioned either by religion, philosophy or democracy—at any rate, suspicious of the mechanistic assumptions—sets up experiments to determine that these microörganisms show a certain amount of judgment and self-determination in their reactions to the stimuli. Child then raises the question as to the effects of various stimuli applied to particular portions of the body surface of the organism. He discovers that the stimulation is not transmitted in full force from the point of contact, and proceeds to structuralize the organism at will by the differential application of stimuli.

In all of this, there is no formal attention to method but the use of some imagination or mind from point to point. The operator raises the question, at appropriate points, "What if," and prepares a set-up to test this query.

Similarly, in our own line, some of us, in connection with some experience, raised a question, "What would happen if we were able to secure life records of a large number of persons which would show their behavior reactions in connection with their various experiences and social situations?" After some experimentation, yourself, Shaw and others have been interested in the preparation of very systematic and elaborate life-histories. In this connection it is noted that the behavior of young persons is dependent upon their social status and the regions in which they live. Studies are then made from the ecological standpoint. It is discovered that children brought into the juvenile court are predominantly from certain localities in the city. The rate of delinquency is related to gang life and gang life is related to localities. Thrasher then makes a study of the gang from this standpoint. As comparative observations multiply, Shaw undertakes to determine how the cases of boys brought into the juvenile court for stealing are connected with their gang life and determines that 90 percent of these boys did their stealing in groups of two or more. In the search for the causes of delinquency, it then appears that the delinquent and nondelinquent are often very much alike in their behavior reactions. It is then recognized that it is impossible to study the delinquent population without at the same time studying the nondelinquent, and at present we have introduced the plan of using nondelinquent groups as a control in connection with studies of the causation of delinquency.

In all this, also, we move from point to point without necessarily any formidable attempt to rationalize and generalize the process. It is only, in fact, so far as sociology is concerned, since we abandoned the search for standardized methods based largely on the work of dead men, that we have made the beginnings which I have indicated.

I think the rest of it isn't so relevant. Here is a formulation, perhaps, which Mr. Thomas still would approve.

MR. THOMAS: I would like to have a copy of that.

MR. BAIN: If the concluding paragraph of Mr. Thomas' rejoinder to Mr. Blumer's appraisal were added to that statement, we would have a better presentation of the position for which I have been contending than I have been able to make.

MR. LERNER: I still want to know what are the tests of the validity of this particular social theory you have just read. It is a social theory that seeks to explain the growth of a body of social ideas, but how do we know it is valid?

MR. STOUFFER: I am not sure, Mr. Chairman, that a question I wanted to raise some time ago is relevant at this point in the discussion. If you feel it isn't, please stop me.

Mr. Blumer ended his introductory remarks this morning by proposing a dilemma. The first part of his dilemma was that sociological knowledge must involve an adequate understanding of the meaning of an event to the individual, and therefore, must be of a psychological character. The second part was that we can't get that knowledge reliably.

It seems to me that in our discussion today we have taken the first part of this alleged dilemma more or less for granted. I agree without any question that it is valuable to get all the psychological insights into any social problem that we can, but it also seems to me that *The Polish Peasant* may have had an unfortunate influence if it has led to an overemphasis upon the necessity of using psychological material explicitly in order to arrive at useful and possibly valid generalizations.

I should like to suggest that nonpsychological study may also lead to useful and valid sociological generalizations, e.g., work of a more or less actuarial character in connection with sociological material such as the work of Burgess, Vold, Glueck, and others, in forecasting the success or failure of prisoners on parole. Another rather interesting example on which there are good data, is trying to decide the probability that a member of a particular class will become an embezzler.

The procedure for arriving at more and more precision is simply this. First, you have a group of 10,000 people exposed to risk as embezzlers, i.e., bonded by a bonding company. Suppose 500 embezzle; you know the probability is 500 out of 10,000 of any persons taken as members of that class being embezzlers.

To get greater predictive precision, instead of considering John Jones as a member of the general class, "population exposed to risk," you limit him by saying he is a member of a subclass, viz., of men twenty to twenty-five exposed to risk; then you can calculate the probability of embezzling by a member of that subclass. Then you make another subclass of such men working in a bank, and so on, *ad finem,* until your data run out.

This type of analysis can be done without explicit reference to the meaning of any of this activity to the individual, and yet you can arrive at fairly valid conclusions or generalizations which are very important for social action—generalizations upon which are based great industries such as bonding and insurance companies.

This kind of sociological study is either ignored or minimized in the type of analysis we have been discussing today. Mr. Blumer properly has stuck to his particular assignment and hasn't considered this other type of analysis but I should like to end my comments by suggesting two things: first, that the type of sociological analysis which makes no explicit reference to the psychological meaning to the subject of the events studied may have great scientific potentiality; and, second, that some phases of the type of inquiry represented by *The Polish Peasant* might very well be carried out by this general method of more or less behavioristic analysis.

The desire in *The Polish Peasant* is to give a picture, as it were, of a whole culture. It would be absurd to expect every element of that culture to be subjected to the very expensive, very meticulous, type of analysis I have described. We can't pay for it—put it that way; and we can't wait for all the elements in an entire culture to be described by that sort of procedure. Therefore, it is valuable for us here today to discuss artistic procedures of acquiring understanding and to appraise concepts conceived in the "grand style." At the same time, we mustn't overlook the importance of this other type

[169]

of analysis which isn't specifically emphasized in such a work as *The Polish Peasant*.

MR. BLUMER: Mr. Chairman, Mr. Thomas is really the one who ought to reply to this comment, but I am going to venture a few remarks myself. Mr. Stouffer is challenging the premise upon which Thomas and Znaniecki have based their work, a premise which to me personally seems sound and genuine. It might be summarized very simply by saying that an individual responds to something in terms of what it means to him. Mr. Thomas' conception is, then, that in the effort to develop a scheme for understanding human behavior, whether individual or collective, it is always necessary to take into consideration this factor of interpretation, or selective choice, by the people whose behavior we are studying. So much for the general statement.

With respect to this specific instance Mr. Stouffer mentions, I should like to say that in terms of Thomas and Znaniecki, the real question is why does a man in a bank respond to the factors around him by committing embezzlement? To get an adequate understanding of that, you must consider the man's own subjective experience. This becomes all the more important because, by this actuarial method, you never arrive at a statement that is 100 percent accurate. If it is true, then, that you have individuals with the same traits and characteristics in the same situation responding differentially to these influences playing upon them, then it becomes important to introduce this factor of subjective experience which determines how the individual is going to react to these influences.

That, as I understand it, is exactly the thesis which Thomas and Znaniecki have proposed in their work. I should like to have Mr. Thomas comment on that.

MR. THOMAS: What Blumer has said represents perfectly my state of mind at the time I was working with Polish materials, but after making seven visits to Sweden and having the benefit of some contacts with Stouffer and others of his kind I realize that the value of a study made with the approach which I was able to use would be greatly increased if Stouffer's approach also were made a feature of it. On the other hand, I have said to him and to others of his kind that their materials will have far from complete meaning until they are associated with and influenced by records of individual experience, such as life histories.

After all, the Polish materials, even if we had had the idea and the competence, are not well suited to Stouffer's approach. So far as I know, Sweden and Holland would be the best locations for his type of work, and Holland is beginning to be, in some respects, but is not as yet, better than Sweden. The Swedish materials contain every item of information obtainable about every individual who is brought before a commission or committed to an institution for investigation. The Swedish state knows where every individual is at every moment from birth to death. If one disappears, they put his name in a record called the "Book of the Nonexistent," until they find him. They have not only a periodic census, but a continuous one. Stouffer mentioned embezzlement. Now, embezzlement is twenty times as frequent today in Sweden as in 1900, and an examination of embezzlement from Stouffer's standpoint would be supported by the kind of records I have indicated. And so with other items.

MR. ALLPORT: How do you plan to conceptualize the Swedish material, or is it too early?

MR. THOMAS: I don't think I shall do anything with it. The materials I first mentioned, the records of individuals, are prepared in one of the divisions of the central prison, Långholmen, in Stockholm, or sent there from about fourteen institutions. They send me copies, and it is informative to read them. I am working now on Jewish material, and I shall not conceptualize it extensively.

MR. ALLPORT: I mean would you like to fit it into an improved theoretical system?

MR. THOMAS: Certainly not, if you mean setting up a complete conceptual scheme in advance and attempting to validate it through the materials. I would necessarily start with some concepts but I would modify them and develop others through the use of the materials. I think the concepts in *The Polish Peasant* are essentially good, but I would let the methodological discussion recede into the background. I would follow the points of view in the document read by Wirth and in the statement of Stouffer.

I will also mention that at one time, in connection with American and Swedish associates, I proposed a Swedish study, in which I am no longer interested, which would have combined the skills and approaches of the sociologist, the social psychologist, the economist, the statistician, the demographer, the political scientist, and the historian, some of them combined in the same person. And if and when other studies are planned, in Sweden or elsewhere, this form of approach should be discussed.

MR. ALLPORT: Do you think you would use attitudes and values as polar concepts, for example?

MR. THOMAS: Yes. But each implies the other, and either could be taken as the point of departure.

MR. ALLPORT: Do you think the wish is derived from the value?

MR. THOMAS: I think of the wish and the value as in a process, somewhat as the hen and the egg, neither of them preceding.

And if I may add a word about the wishes (Blumer mercifully refrained from mentioning that there are two different formulations of them in the study), I regard my formulation as a very suggestive scheme to show that the satisfactions men desire (excitement, change, safety, security, affection, distinction, etc.), may be rudely classified. That has some importance for interpretation but it would be unprofitable to specify what attitudes, values, and wishes are reflected in each and all of the concrete acts of behavior examined.

MR. ALLPORT: Then you have a new point of view toward the importance of the psychological factor?

MR. THOMAS: Only in the sense that while I should wish to have psychological concepts in my mind and to use them, I should not give them an exclusive role nor a prominence which would obscure the main purpose. In my course on social attitudes which I had been teaching six or eight years before this study was undertaken, I had been evolving psychological concepts and these were transferred to *The Polish Peasant* along with those of Znaniecki, with the result that, with the exception of young men who are writing text books, everybody who refers to the work pays no attention to the data—to what is going on in the process, to what is happening. I have acquired a certain aversion to the mention of the work on that account. And since I have joined in the depreciation of certain aspects of the work, I may be permitted to say that, whatever else it is, it is a significant piece of historical interpretation. Perhaps it is just that.

CHAIRMAN THOMPSON: Could you have arrived at the conclusions you have expressed, Mr. Thomas, without having written *The Polish Peasant?*

MR. THOMAS: Eventually, perhaps, but it is true that the letter read by Wirth, and which I had forgotten, was a reaction against *The Polish Peasant.*

MR. ALLPORT: People who thought your psychological ideas were inadequate were stimulated to try to improve upon them. They have tried to redefine the concept of attitude because you used it, perhaps, loosely. The same thing can be said about your personality types. Many people who rejected them felt impelled to try to do a better job. That is notoriously true about the wishes.

The psychologists reacted against these ideas very strongly in spite of the fact that many people accepted them. Psychologists were mightily offended and were stimulated thereby to do their own motivational work a little more energetically. One of the greatest successes of the book is the way it has made itself outmoded on the psychological side.

Now if you should conceptualize this material again with the aid of modern psychology, you would find a far more discriminating set of concepts at your disposal. Would you now turn your back on a discriminative and improved psychology, which you indirectly helped to improve, and seek social uniformities by the actuarial or cluster analysis method which Mr. Stouffer mentioned? I take it you would prefer to do that?

MR. THOMAS: No, I would not turn my back on psychology but I do not recognize that its employment is incompatible with Stouffer's approach. Why should it be all or none? That is Blumer's mistake about the validity of the document. He thinks it should be all or none.

MR. LERNER: If you react against all of your own earlier conceptualisms toward simpler formulations, isn't there a danger of running into planless empiricism? How would you escape that?

MR. THOMAS: It is plain that I appreciate a certain employment of concepts, and I am not even sure that there is such a thing as planless empiricism in any form of research.

MR. LERNER: You have no objection to conceptualisms, no matter how ambitious they may be, if they are integrated with the material?

[174]

MR. THOMAS: No. I think there should be complete freedom in respect to that.

MR. NICHOLS: Mr. Thomas' explanation of his own experience is closely followed, I think, by certain developments in the historian's profession. I suppose it is a coincidence, but a very interesting one, that your book came out just about the time that certain historians were becoming converted to a more humble idea of history. Your book is really a plea to the sociologists to take into account certain historical methods, and about that time certain social historians in this country were beginning to use just the sort of documents that you were making use of. Instead of attempting to work out extraordinarily involved dynamics and theories of human development or economic interpretation, they were getting down to earth and trying to see what people actually were doing. Of course, they had been struggling for two hundred years or more with documents and had developed an enormously complex technic for dealing with them. But since about 1920, I think we have followed certain methods which you suggested; we also are now turning to our psychological and sociological brethren for help. In other words, the documents must be interpreted, not only according to rules of truth and justice and accuracy, and so on, but also according to the best information we can get from the psychologists and sociologists as to human behavior; these documents must be related to their social patterns. We haven't gotten very far with it.

MR. LERNER: I think it is worth saying, too, that the tendency of the historian to turn to the so-called "social," to what men are actually doing, finally trivialized the whole conception of social history. Historical research became synonymous with finding out how many sewing machines or phonographs people had and defining social in that sense. The whole

[175]

tendency was to move away from conceptualism toward the so-called objective factor.

MR. NICHOLS: Isn't that a necessary step, though? We have to get away from certain of the old things. By detailed, specific researches in social history, we can create a new body of data from which we can derive new and more valid generalizations. We have learned a great many things which I hope will make possible a more realistic synthesis of the evolution of human behavior. We shall not merely *describe* the objective development of certain states and institutions, but shall *explain* it in terms of the basic social patterns of behavior which underlie such development. This book under review, of course, is an excellent historical document from this point of view. It gives concrete illustrations of the experiences of a group of people who left one environment and came over to another, with attempted explanations of why they behaved as they did. The whole tendency, it seems to me, not only in sociology and history, but also in other disciplines, is to bring research down to earth in terms of actual human behavior.

MR. BAIN: In other words, you think the historians actually are doing what Mr. Lerner seemed to deplore when it was referred to a while ago, i.e., doing the many million man-hours of research on specific, carefully delimited problems which, additively, does constitute a realistic basis for historical synthesis. In other words, it is necessary to know how many sewing machines people use in a particular area at a particular time; it is really the kind of knowledge which keeps history from being merely a literary, or dramatic, or nonfactual discipline.

MR. NICHOLS: Yes, we are beginning to count according to Mr. Stouffer's idea. Whether we will get eventually to using machines and punch-cards, and so on, I don't know. Some of us are working on that.

MR. LERNER: I wasn't criticizing the counting of sewing machines. I think it is worth while.

MR. NICHOLS: No, he is criticizing the piling up of a lot of things without making anything out of them.

MR. BAIN: You can't make anything out of anything until you have done some proper piling up.

MR. LERNER: We go on accumulating millions and millions of man-hours of information about these things but we still have the problem of making that synthesis.

MR. NICHOLS: That is true, but we have broken down some old syntheses which we no longer believe in.

MR. LERNER: They may have been good syntheses.

MR. WIRTH: You may be confusing good syntheses or plausible theories about history and social life, to which parties have attached themselves and which so frequently have become fighting words.

MR. LERNER: Here we have the empirical data, here we have the abstraction into which we are attempting to fit them. Modify the abstraction to fit the data and go and collect more data to fit the new abstraction; there is a constant interaction between them. It is only when one goes off in one direction or the other that there is danger. Whether this interaction between these two poles of scientific inquiry will lead us to more tenable generalizations, I do not think has been demonstrated as yet. If it isn't the proper way, at least no one has yet suggested any other way of getting general truths.

MR. BAIN: I think Mr. Allport's remarks certainly illustrated that. Here was the Methodological Note, an afterthought not logically integrated with the materials at all, just thrown out by the authors, but it became a very productive stimulus which induced men to study many simple, specific, carefully formulated problems susceptible of empirical verification. Darwin's theory had a similar history. Perhaps one of the major functions of social theorists is to set up grand hypotheses which, while being knocked to pieces, produce new valid scientific knowledge which later can be integrated into a more coherent and consistent general theory. Certainly, the theories of Herbert Spencer, with now only a few battered, tattered shreds of them left intact—had a tremendous influence in developing whatever sociology there is. Darwin's theory had a similar fate and performed a similar function for biology. I think it could be pretty well shown that the major contribution of every grandiose social theory that makes a contribution at all is to stimulate meticulous, laborious, unromantic man-hours of work on small, simplified problems which eventually makes possible—rather, compels—a new theoretical synthesis.

MR. ALLPORT: I think you are too optimistic. We can easily be too optimistic about these new syntheses. We have had experience enough now to know that whenever we tear down a grand myth, Spencerian or a Marxian, and try to synthesize on the basis of the empirical studies by which they were torn down, we get a whole crop of possible conceptualizations. We still haven't answered our question as to the criterion for a valid conceptualization.

MR. NICHOLS: Have you an answer, Mr. Lerner?

MR. LERNER: No, I have no answer. I am exploring the difficulty of getting an answer. I think we have been a little too optimistic on other matters. For example, Mr. Bain spoke of the usefulness of finding out about sewing machines. It probably was, but I think what really happened was a reaction against political history from the introduction of certain hypotheses of a general character like the economic hypothesis, materialistic hypothesis, and so on. The historian now felt called upon to explore social attitudes rather than military or political behavior. He found it very difficult to find material bearing on genuine social attitudes but relatively easy to count sewing machines. Here were very empirical data which could be tabulated. Such a problem is amenable to this kind of man-hour work, but its significance is questionable. It isn't an accident that social history disintegrated.

MR. BAIN: We can't tell how significant a newly found fact may be. About twenty-five years ago, a man found out that some angleworms have higher I.Q.'s than others. This was one of those atomistic researches which you might think has no significance, though this one happened to be very important. Most such researches may not be of much significance *per se,* but the progress of science in every field has been largely due to these chance observations, or apparently unrelated discoveries. If these seeming insignificant and unimportant facts are inconsistent with the present accepted theory, they may later become crucial factors in the reformulation of new theory. If they are within the present framework, they have an additive value for the verification of the theory.

MR. NICHOLS: Another thing the social history has done is to create a good deal of intellectual dissatisfaction among people which is a stimulus to further work.

MR. WALLER: Actually a good many different organizing hypotheses have emerged over a period of fifty years. Admittedly, most empirical researches have had little value, but every once in a while somebody produces an organizing idea which enables us to fit many of the apparently useless empirical facts into a configuration so that they make sense.

MR. MURDOCK: If there hadn't been a lot of pigeon fanciers and horse breeders and so on, Darwin wouldn't have had the material to make his concept.

MR. STOUFFER: It seems to me it is equally important for us to have respect for the value of tools. There is a tendency to sneer at the toolmaker as well as at the person who is doing a rather meticulous piece of work. I recently read Shryock's *The History of Medicine,* and was impressed by the fact that there we find concepts, theories, and so on, but we also find things like microscopes. The men who invented and improved the microscope were probably of more importance to the development of scientific medicine than were all the men who were thinking and talking about medical theories from Galen to Pasteur. The same is true of many other aspects of medical technology. We tend to neglect this, to dismiss it as something that will just take care of itself. We want verbal and logical tests of grand ideas. I think if all the best thinkers living in the 16th century had concentrated their thought on explaining the problems of medicine—what was "true," or "valid," about medical theories—they wouldn't have got anywhere, or very far.

To use a favorite sentence of Professor Ogburn's, any invention is based upon a supporting frequency distribution of previous inventions. I doubt very much whether we can make much progress in developing generalizations of very high probability until we get much more accurate ways of testing them. We must invent sociological instruments of precision. I think Thomas' *Polish Peasant* may have deflected the attention of some sociologists away from the development of the precision procedures which are so important. I say this without in the slightest trying to minimize the importance of any and all procedures that will give us hunches and insights. They are useful in every stage of research—and particularly useful in helping us to choose significant problems capable of precise empirical test.

MR. ALLPORT: There is one danger in your position, viz., that we may come to deify a planless empiricism. There seems to be a tendency to do just that in modern operationalism. It is a form of skepticism that is fatal for conceptualization. In the absence of the "grand style" hypothesis, or at least, a "modest style," empiricism is worthless.

MR. LERNER: The German culture, in which precision procedures have been developed most highly in science, is today in complete catastrophe when judged by criteria which I think most of us would accept as valid. Germany achieved high development both in abstract social thought and in the precision procedures of natural science, but the latter did not preserve the social values in that culture. I do not underestimate the value of precision procedures, but I think Germany offers a good illustration of what happens in a culture when precision procedures are made objectives in themselves.

MR. STOUFFER: Today, we do not have the necessary precision procedures with which to study culture, and probably will not have for a long time to come—except for very small cultural segments. In the meantime, we need all the descriptive and interpretative studies we can get, using all the non-precision methods we can devise. If there is one point on which everybody here today will agree, surely it is that. However, when we chart the future of social science research, I think it is certain that one of the most important developments will be toward rephrasing our hypotheses in language which is predetermined by better tools for verification. There fore, I think far more importance should be attached to precision procedures as a method of formulating and verifying hypotheses than Mr. Blumer has done in his appraisal of *The Polish Peasant*.

Of course, we cannot answer big, vague, world-girdling questions, such as Mr. Lerner's theory of why Germany is in its present state, by precision procedures. Such general questions are beyond precision procedures; they probably can't be answered by any method. They may be vitally important, but they are the wrong kind of questions for scientific research at the present stage. We expect too much immediately from our science with its present instruments and methods. We must realize that we are decades behind some of the other sciences, e.g., there are many thousands of published researches each year in the one little field which deals with the pituitary gland. Possibly less than a hundred researches of permanent scientific value are published each year in the whole domain of sociology. We are just beginning. No wonder the Germans paid little attention to the product of the social sciences!

Mr. BAIN: Mr. Lerner seemed to imply that Germany is in its present state because it had such a high development of precision instruments and procedures. One could turn the argument around just as well and point out that the Germans have been most productive of elaborate, abstract, world-girdling social theories and have done very little with precision procedures in this field.

Mr. LERNER: I didn't mean to imply what you have just said. I mentioned their vast development of abstract social theory. If there was any implication, it is that these precision procedures did not save the German system of social thought.

Mr. BAIN: Neither did the development of these vast verbal abstractions. The significant thing is that there were no precision procedures for analyzing social phenomena; for physical and biological phenomena, there were—and the Germans are still doing pretty well in these fields.

Mr. LERNER: I think we are agreed neither by itself is adequate. I would like to venture one of those vast world-girdling guesses that don't mean anything—sheer conjecture. I think the same culture that develops vast and meaningless abstractions is also likely to develop almost equally meaningless precision procedures. American culture is a good illustration. We turn out of our universities people who are specialized in abstract thought, but they have little definite knowledge of the relationship between that abstract thought and the realm of social action. We also turn out highly trained technicians, engineers and scientists, who have no genuine understanding of the relationship between their technics and social objectives.

The result is the spread of the same kind of irrationalism among the young men in our culture as was the case in Germany. This suggests the necessity for an organic view, which we have not developed any more than Germany did. In other words, it is a plea for synthesis, not of abstractions only, but between abstractions and operative realities.

MR. BAIN: I think we all would agree to that.

MR. WALLER: One thing that strikes me in all this discussion is the remarkable degree of unanimity. I expected to see much sharper divergences of opinion than have actually developed. Most of the fundamental points of the analysis that Blumer has given us have not even been discussed; they have been accepted.

MR. BAIN: There is great unanimity that Blumer has done a fine job; everybody will agree to that. There is unanimity that *The Polish Peasant* has played an important part in the development of such sociology as we have. Beyond that, it seems to me that there are at least three or four very definitely divergent points of view. I don't know whether I could identify them at the moment, but I think I disagree with Mr. Lerner on most points, and agree fairly well with Mr. Wirth.

MR. WIRTH: On the other hand, I find myself in great agreement with Lerner on most of his points. (*Laughter*).

MR. BAIN: I think there is unanimous agreement on only two points, first, that *The Polish Peasant* has had a great influence and is a milestone in the history of sociology; second, that Blumer's analysis is a masterly piece of work. Beyond that there are several distinctly different points of view about such fundamental things as the nature of social phenomena, the methods by which they can be studied, the possibility of scientific laws describing social data, and the testing of generalizations. I don't believe the Committee or anybody else can find out, from studying this record at any rate, what are the criteria of significant work in the social sciences. There are several views about that—certainly no great unanimity has been manifested here.

MR. NOURSE: Should any further steps be taken? We have agreed that publication is desirable. Is there anything else?

MR. THOMAS: It has been my experience in situations like this that the person who has expressed himself may want to rephrase himself or edit himself. That should be understood. There must be a good deal of waste in what we all have said.

CHAIRMAN THOMPSON: Certainly; nothing will be printed until the speakers have given their approval, Mr. Thomas. I want to express on behalf of the Committee, our very great appreciation of the time and trouble you have taken to attend this conference and add to it. We are stumbling around in the dark, as you realize, but I hope we won't stumble quite so much after this, thanks to you gentlemen.

If there is nothing further, we will adjourn.

SUPPLEMENTARY STATEMENT BY GORDON W. ALLPORT

It was an excellent conference, largely because of its concentration upon the central question posed by Max Lerner right at the start: *How do we know when we have a valid social theory?* During the discussion, many possible criteria were examined by the conferees: (1) sheer illuminative power; (2) squaring with other extant theories; (3) internal consistency of all the parts of the theory; (4) conformity with known facts; (5) predictive power; (6) pragmatic value; (7)

endorsement by experts; (8) its conformity with basic postulates.

Although weaknesses were found in most of these criteria, taken together they make a fairly promising array and can be used by the individual scientist to solve this problem in his own way according to the canons of logic that he customarily employs.

Among the criteria listed above, the one that intrigues me most is that concerning the predictive power of a theory, but it seems to me that the argument for prediction is bedeviled by a failure to recognize two kinds of prediction: (a) actuarial prediction concerning whole populations of people and (b) individual prediction concerning the possibilities of action for a single person. Social scientists have confused the probability of action within a population with the probability of what a *given* individual will do. To say that 70 percent of the population will go to the moving pictures this week does not mean that any given individual has a 70 percent chance of going. To say that 50 percent of the cases fall within one PE of a mean is not to say that a given individual has a 50 percent chance of falling within this range. To know what his chance is we must study *him*.

The range of variability is not primarily a psychological problem but an actuarial problem. The displacement of the psychological point of view by the actuarial point of view is the chief fallacy of statistical social science. It leads to psychological absent-mindedness. We are really positing a mass mind when we speak of probability in this way.

The only way in which we can predict the chances that a given individual has of behaving in a certain way is to study him as an individual and especially his subjective mental processes with the aid of subjective categories. Part of the influence of *The Polish Peasant* is due to its implicit recogni-

[185]

tion of this distinction between two types of prediction and its concentration upon the predictive posers of life history documents.

SUPPLEMENTARY STATEMENT BY GEORGE P. MURDOCK

I am not so sure that we went as far as we might have in appraising *The Polish Peasant*. Lerner, in particular, it seemed to me, bent the discussion in the direction of criteria of validity and general methodology in the social sciences— that mare's nest of argument wherever social scientists are assembled—and away from a specific analysis of the work in question. There were several points which I should have liked to bring up had the discussion turned in that direction. Perhaps I may summarize them here.

Thomas and Znaniecki's work was significant for its departure from the meliorism and philosophizing of previous sociology in the direction of a scientific orientation. They abandoned instinctivism and paved the way for a socially useful conception of impulses. They adopted the conception of culture and its regional differentiation which had been worked out by the anthropologist and, unlike Sumner, who had anticipated them in this respect, applied this perspective to materials which sociologists commonly regard as distinctively theirs. In so doing, however, like the anthropologists, they tended to assume culture patterns as historically given and failed fully to recognize the extent to which they represent solutions to man's animal and societal needs produced through a long process of adaptation. Culture change is viewed, rather, as the product of interacting values and attitudes. This minimizes too greatly, it seems to me, the imperative nature of man's biological equipment, which cultures are compelled to cope with.

[186]

They deserve great credit for introducing sociologists to the use of human documents. The growing recent interest in so-called "culture and personality" studies goes back, directly or indirectly, in large measure to them. In their use of human documents, however, they seem to me to lay altogether too little stress upon the early formative years of the life history, when the animal is undergoing social conditioning, when the foundations of character are being laid down, when, in short, the fundamental "attitudes" effective in later life are being formed. Irrespective of one's psychological predilections, whether Freudian or behavioristic, the earliest years in the life of the individual seem to deserve the most intensive study on the part of those seeking to integrate cultural and personality data.

As for the rest, I find myself in wholehearted agreement with Blumer's comprehensive and penetrating analysis.

SUPPLEMENTARY STATEMENT BY MALCOLM M. WILLEY

These comments, added three months after the conference, represent a residual impression. There were two points of view that, in my judgment, might appropriately have been introduced into the conference for elaboration and further discussion. The fact they were not given proper weight led, I feel, to some degree of onesidedness.

1. There was no clearcut statement of the position that the methodology of the social sciences must or should be the methodology that has developed in the natural sciences. Presumably, the exponent of this argument would deny not only the significance but the utility of such nonmeasurable concepts as "values." Surely he would rule out from consideration "observers' " judgments; in short, he would deny that consideration of the subjective on what is largely a de-

scriptive or subjective basis can lead to development of sociology as a science. To one who takes such a position, there can be in methodology no essential or fundamental distinction between *social science* and *natural science*. Accordingly, the point would be advanced that Thomas and Znaniecki have not developed a scheme that constitutes a basic structure for the scientific study of social life or for the development of a scientific social theory. To talk of the authors' methods as scientific is in the same category, it would be argued, as talking of scientific religion. It would have rounded the entire discussion to have had a forceful presentation of this point of view—a point of view that necessarily is abbreviated in description here almost to the point of caricature. Yet it is a point that may be effectively developed, as the literature of sociology shows.

2. This leads naturally to the second point which, in my opinion, was underdeveloped in the discussion. It was Stouffer who introduced the idea that even within the framework that the Methodological Note created, it might be possible to use statistical procedures in the analysis of the problems that were under consideration. Thomas and Znaniecki are not quantitative in their approach, nor do they attempt to check their assumptions or establish their hypothesis by induction. But does it follow that statistical procedures are without their uses in dealing with the problems? Is there no way in which the realm of values can be invaded by more exact methods? Are sociologists unable to push their "science" beyond a reliance upon subjective judgments? Or are problems in sociology by their very nature incapable of analysis on other than descriptive bases and hence essentially nonscientific? Such points cannot be elaborated here but they are relevant to Blumer's analysis and might well have been given more attention at the conference.

The keenness of Blumer's analysis throughout cannot be gainsaid. It is profound and stimulating at the same time. If it is subject to criticism, it might be on the ground that Blumer tends to take a somewhat too rigid "either-or" position. This, it seems to me, is evident in the discussion of social laws. Blumer points out, and correctly, that Thomas and Znaniecki do not actually formulate the social laws which were their objective. It was certainly incumbent upon Blumer to point out this shortcoming in the authors' scheme; and yet I am not certain that this weakness is as vital as Blumer would appear to make it. My point may perhaps be clarified by turning to pages 27-28 of Blumer's analysis. Here he writes:

> This last point should be made clear. As we have mentioned previously, the methodological approach proposed by Thomas and Znaniecki can and must be viewed on two levels. The first level merely represents the general realization that in social life the influence of cultural and objective factors is dependent on the disposition of individuals and that, consequently, this subjective factor enters into the social life as a vital aspect that cannot be ignored. The second level of the conception takes the form of presupposing that the relation between the objective and the subjective factors is of the definite sort that is asserted by the methodological formula. Even though the second conception may be invalid, the first may be valid. Indeed, this seems to be the case. On logical grounds, the methodological formula as a device for securing laws of social becoming is fallacious; the fact that it is not seriously employed by the authors is further evidence of this.

Is there not between the two levels described by Blumer an intermediate level upon which one may work? Is there not between the level that recognizes in broad manner that certain relationships prevail and the level of precise formulation of specific "laws of social becoming," an area in which relationships may be established, at least upon a tentative basis,— relationships that will serve as next-steps leading to the more precise social laws for which the authors and Blumer and all sociologists are seeking? To my mind, failure to stress the importance of this intermediate level of conception, and it is the level on which Thomas and Znaniecki appear to me to have been working, is to ignore in some measure the importance of the contribution that was made in *The Polish Peasant*.

This leads into my final point. There was considerable discussion at the conference that came perilously close to hair-splitting. Some of this took the form of a demand for some absolute logical consistency on the part of the authors and upon the part of the analyst. Inconsistency or lack of logic, to be sure, are not to be commended, especially if they represent carelessness of definition or intellectual laziness. At the same time, in developing a plan for social research, there is a real danger that one may become so engrossed in his details of logic that he fails to enter upon those studies and researches that will, through their conclusions, lead to the logical refinements that underlie the development of any science.

What I am trying to say is that adherence to a standard of logical perfection in the development of any research methodology or in the elaboration of an intellectual framework within which research is to be carried forward, may serve to impede progress in research rather than contribute to it. There is such a thing as confusing logical perfection with practical necessities. I would argue that it is possible to make advances in social science even though every step is not logical to the degree that some of the discussion at the conference would seem to call for. A science grows bit by bit, through a process of moving ahead and back-tracking. A science could die stillborn as the result of a demand for logical perfection in the framework before taking any of the steps that lead to concrete attack upon specific problems. A plea for perfectionism may get the research worker nowhere. And so it seems to me that any attitude of logical defeatism is to be guarded against. Such studies as Blumer's and that of

Thomas and Znaniecki ought to stimulate the research worker and not lead to a consciousness of logical imperfection that inhibits all advance.

SUMMARY AND ANALYSIS OF CONFERENCE BY READ BAIN

The Committee thought it might be useful to have a summary statement of the work accomplished by the Conference on Blumer's *Appraisal* of Thomas and Znaniecki's *The Polish Peasant*. Since I edited the transcription of the discussion, it was suggested that I prepare such a statement, giving in addition my general impressions of the whole proceedings. This is a shortened ("general impressions" deleted) and slightly amended version of my report to the Committee.

Three things stand out. First, there was unanimous agreement that Blumer had produced a work of permanent methodological value in his *Appraisal* and that it, with the statements of Thomas and Znaniecki, should be published. These constitute Part I of this volume.

Second, there was unanimous agreement that *The Polish Peasant* is a notable contribution to sociology although its avowed purpose of finding "social laws of becoming" was not realized and its conceptual scheme of *attitudes, values, wishes,* resultant *personality types,* and *definitions of situations,* does not seem to be capable of producing such laws. It was agreed that this conceptual scheme was not and cannot be derived logically from the documents, nor proved by them, although the documents are greatly illuminated when interpreted according to the scheme, and correspondingly, the scheme is made more plausible, and thus perhaps is partially "verified," by the use the authors have made of documents. It was generally agreed, however, that some of the subsidiary generalizations, such as the theory of personal and social disorganization and reorganization resulting from the clash of cultures, have been of practical use to social workers dealing with immigrants, to students of crime, and to others dealing with social problems. It was also agreed that this work has had a great stimulating and fertilizing influence upon the subsequent development of sociology, particularly in the use of human document material, as well as upon the use of similar techniques in adjacent fields such as history, anthropology, and psychology. It was generally agreed that *The Polish Peasant* is a monumental instance of the revolt against "armchair" sociology which began about 1900 and has progressed to such an extent that sociologists increasingly regard themselves as natural scientists. Few present day sociological theorists fail to give lip-service, at least, to this conception of sociology and they also profess to base their theories upon actual or possible empirical research. There appears to be some recession from this point of view in recent years, perhaps due to influences from Europe where sociology has been, and still is to a considerable extent, less an empirical discipline than a logico-philosophical one, depending for its data largely upon history, anthropology and common sense.

One of the chief contributions of *The Polish Peasant* appears to be its great influence in turning sociologists toward concrete, empirical investigations which employ large masses of data which can be used by subsequent investigators. It also emphasizes the idea that social phenomena are natural phenomena, that they all have a "natural history," and that the investigator must not have a moralistic, i.e., must have a natural science, point of view and habit of mind. Whatever his methods and theories may be, they must be relevant to the data, and his conclusions must grow out of the research and be relevant to it. Most Conference members would probably agree that moral or ideological factors are usually involved in the selection of research problems, and perhaps in the conduct of the research and the presentation both of data and findings. For example, Thomas and Znaniecki "found out about" some aspects of Polish peasant life which they could not print. In certain tabooed areas of human behavior, all sociologists and social psychologists know it is very difficult to do research at all, and still more difficult to publish the results. However, what is meant by the nonmoralistic attitude of science is that after the problem has been chosen and defined, then ideological predispositions must not interfere with the collection of data, analysis, and a full presentation of the findings. This is the ideology of science, its moral frame of reference, viz., that it shall not be swayed by any nonscientific values from honest and exhaustive investigation and unambiguous, unequivocal presentation of its findings. Its assumptions and procedures must be made sufficiently explicit so that other investigators may repeat the analysis of the same or similar data.

Third, it was generally agreed that because Blumer stuck so closely to the task assigned by the Committee, viz., an attempt to answer the questions—What was the purpose of this work? How successfully was it achieved? How were data and methods employed? How useful would they be for further research in this field? What generalizations were reached? Are they sound deductions from the data? Were there any recommendations for social action, and if so, were they proper conclusions from the data?—he necessarily failed to present many ideas which are pertinent to the general problem of evaluating research in the social sciences. There was considerable consensus that some of these were brought out in the Conference and, therefore, that a condensed and amended version of this discussion might be printed profitably along with Blumer's *Appraisal* and Thomas' and Znaniecki's *statements*.

A great deal of the discussion centered around the problem of how we can verify or validate theoretical propositions formulated to "explain" social phenomena. Very wide differences of opinion on this were expressed. They ranged from the belief that social laws with the degree of invariance and predictive power to which we are accustomed in the physical and biological sciences are impossible in the social sciences, to the view that they are possible and that some actually exist, particularly in economics, and that the logic and method of formulating such laws are the same in the social as in the physical and biological sciences.

The first view emphasizes the idea that social phenomena always involve certain aspects which have been called the "subjective factor", i.e., in the Thomas-Znaniecki scheme, the "attitudes," biologically "given" and/or culturally imposed and conditioned, which "determine" response to a given social situation. One's response must always be in terms of what the stimulus (defined situation) "means"—which always will be relative to one's "values." This is the "subjective element" which is the distinctive characteristic of social phenomena. Presumably, it is an element which is lacking in all physical response (reaction is more appropriate) and also in all biological responses except those of the so-called "higher" organisms. Certainly, the fact that man is conditioned by and to an elaborate symbolic (cultural) environment which in a sense transcends both time and space, makes this subjective factor of great importance. Even granting that such responses, whether symbolized or not, are merely neuro-muscular, and are causally determined and habitual, the fact that they are so numerous, overlapping, and interactive produces an instability, unpredictability, and uniqueness, the ignoring of which, as is usually though perhaps not necessarily done by statistical procedures, destroys the essential quality and character of the data themselves. The "meaning of a situation" to a *person* is a personal, subjective, unique, differential datum. To "understand" this requires some degree of imaginative insight (based on past experience, of course), or empathic identification. To formulate "laws of becoming" which are useful for social control, this "subjective" factor, the "meaning of the situation" to the subject, cannot be ignored. The kind of prediction that is important is "What will *This Subject* do in this given situation?" Therefore, social "laws" can be suggestive, plausible, and perhaps useful, but cannot be definitive and invariable when applied to the behavior of particular subjects, which is what we want for prediction and control.

The other point of view emphasizes the idea that laws are possible because there is considerable uniformity and permanence in the occurrence of observed and observable social phenomena, whether they be called "objective" or "subjective." It believes that we have ample evidence to warrant such a position. It points out that in the physical and biological realms, there are a great many observable phenomena which are, or appear to be, so instable (what Giddings called "turbulences") that invariant laws are impossible; and also that all physical and biological laws are formulated in terms of probability, within carefully defined limits, by operations which involve only a few carefully defined variables—highly abstracted, and therefore controllable; and further, that the behavior of units in such systems is never identical with their theoretically predicted behavior. In many cases, differential behavior of the units is completely unobservable as in the case of molecules, atoms, and electrons, and yet there is every reason to infer that such differential behavior actually occurs, just as it does in all cases where differential unit-behavior is observable.

It seemed to me about four theoretical positions were expressed which would fall within the limits of the two polaric views stated above. For the purpose of brief presentation, I have called them theories of: 1. Illuminative insight; 2. Organizing concepts; 3. Logico-systematic analysis; and 4. Delimited empirical research. These all may be conceived as modes of ordering, or in a loose sense, "explaining," those behaviors variously called social, societal, or cultural. They differ somewhat in methods of procedure, degree of verifiability, amount and kind of abstraction involved, and, possibly, in their conceptions of the nature of social phenomena. All of them have this in common, however: they are trying to make some kind of "sense" out of social phenomena; implicitly, at least, all are striving to increase man's rational control over the social phenomena of which he is a part. All are therefore ratiocinative rather than experiential; all must deal with symbols of actually observed or inferred social data. In this sense, all four are abstract and "subjective," but since man "knows" social objects in the same way that he knows physical objects, i.e., by responding to them similarly, such responses being mediated by symbols before any kind of communicable generalizations are possible, all four positions are also abstract and "objective." "Objective" is thus taken to mean "capable of being communicated symbolically." As Russell has said, "subjective" is private, "objective" is public. These terms are therefore matters of degree, since anything "completely subjective" could never be "known" at all; it could merely be *experienced* by the subject.

The first position holds that research in the social sciences proceeds by insight and "hunches." It gives us generalizations which can be called plausible but not provable. We "recognize" their "validity" by a strong subjective feeling—"This is true! It gives me a better understanding; it 'sheds light' upon these data." Our feeling is somewhat like our response to a work of art which "gets us," except we are dealing with abstracted data further removed from immediate, unique, sensory experience than is true of "literary or esthetic illumination." It is held that this is the only kind of generalizations we can make regarding that type of phenomena designated by "attitude" in *The Polish Peasant*—especially, when those attitudes are manifested in "becoming situations" such as are involved in transitional cultures, whether the transition is *between* cultures, as when a peasant moves from Poland to Chicago, or *within* cultures, as when farm boys go to the city, or when new technological devices introduce rapid and extensive changes into the culture. Needless to say, such generalizations may be "useful" in both personal and societal practical affairs. To this extent, they may be called, pragmatically, both "true" and "scientific." Needless to say, also, such illuminative formulations are likely to be made by men who have wide, intimate, personal experience with the involved data—if they also have the rare quality we call "creative or constructive imagination." This is what social workers mean by "natural fixers" and what we mean by saying that certain people are "good judges of character" and have an "intuitive understanding of human nature." This is probably what Cooley meant by saying Goethe might have been a very great sociologist.

The second position is somewhat similar, except it is a mode of organizing or relating a great many data under a very general conceptual scheme. Here also, "creative" imagination is involved but it is more systematic and inclusive than the mere illuminating interpretation of a rather limited body of material in a more or less restricted field. Examples of such organizing concepts, I suppose, would be Comte's and Spencer's systems, the theories of Marx and Freud, and somewhat more limited but still comprehensive enough to be placed here, such ideas as Tarde's regarding imitation, Durkheim's about collective representations, Sumner's on folkways, Pareto's on residues and derivations, Cooley's on primary and secondary group behavior and the "tentative organic process," and probably the Thomas-Znaniecki scheme of attitude-value-wish. This is still generalization by insight and hunch, but it is in the "grand style." Its validity and usefulness depends largely upon the degree of "illumination" it sheds upon the data to which it purports to refer. Certainly, such generalizing is much more abstract, farther removed from mere literary insight, and more concerned with immediate and specific instances than ordinary "illuminating interpretations." Such organizing concepts apparently have their origin in the accumulation of considerable common-sense knowledge, historical incident, or more or less careful observation, and empirically derived facts.

The history of such all-inclusive theories to date is that all of them are relatively inadequate. However, they give rise to many specific researches in the fields they attempt to organize; this vastly increases the sum total of human knowledge and ends by destroying the concepts as originally stated. Few of them are actually disproved; they are just forgotten, or else are restated so as to become more denotative and less connotative. The history of the Ptolemaic, Copernican, Keplerian, Newtonian, and Einsteinian theories might be instanced; or the Greeks, Lamarck, E. and C. Darwin, down to modern organic evolutionary theory. In the social sciences, such inclusive theories appear to be suggestive and stimulating rather than definitive and demonstrative. They give plausible and meaningful ways of viewing vast bodies of data, many of which are highly suspect, rather than dependable, verified, scientific knowledge. However, they are fruitful in that they do stimulate careful and refined researches and, during their "period of vitality," furnish concepts of practical utility to man in his struggle to organize his chaos of experience. They are defective in that they frequently take on the character of cults and become the rallying cries of uncritical proponents of doubtful "causes." The use (or misuse) of the Four Wishes furnishes a good illustration. Freudian repression, the "only child," supply and demand, instincts, the economic man, inferiority feelings, etc., are other examples. However, even sound scientific knowledge in any field is not immune from such use and abuse. The Devil always has quoted Scripture.

The third point of view may be thought of as one way of testing the "validity" of such organizing concepts as those above. It is also applicable to the evaluation of any empirical research however carefully delimited. It is the specialty of the theorist. It attempts to test the methods of the research man, his conclusions, and his recommendations, by *thinking about them* as critically, comprehensively and comprehendingly, exhaustively and intensively, as is humanly possible. This function is in some disrepute in these days when prestige and acclaim are attached to the empirical investigator. Such logico-systematic analysis must be done in an "armchair." By its very nature, it is highly abstract, and also highly productive. Einstein uses an armchair. A man in an armchair—*with brains*—is a combination indispensable to science.

To do this work well requires a type of mind far rarer than the kind of mind that can do valuable empirical research. Occasionally, an individual may possess both capacities to a high degree. Such a person leaves a notable record in the annals of science. To be equipped for it, one has to be familiar with the history, methods, findings, and practical applications of science in both his own and adjacent fields, and the circle of adjacency expands to include all the natural sciences. He must be an expert logician, a man of wide information and creative imagination. He tries to lay bare the implicit postulates of the work under consideration and to test them by seeing what the result would be if these data, generalizations, and inferences were based upon a different set of postulates; he tries to see if the system presented is internally consistent; if it is consistent with other relevant scientific knowledge; if it is as simple and inclusive as it logically can be; if there are any valid "negative cases"; if other equally logical interpretations of the data are possible; and so on.

This is a mode of testing propositions, but it also is often productive of propositions to be tested. Some capacity of this sort would prevent a good many "empirical researches" from making themselves and empirical research as ridiculous as they frequently do. A few competent men of this kind on the staff of all large research projects might lessen the waste of research foundation funds and hasten the achievement of sound research in the social sciences. Most research eventually gets this logico-systematic analysis *after it has been completed;* it also should get it *before it is done;* if this procedure were followed, much of it would never be done at all, or would be very differently done, instead of being done indifferently as is now so often the case. Also, the charge of "planless and pointless empiricism" would not be so common—nor so just.

The fourth point of view brings us to the opposite pole from "illuminative insight." It emphasizes the necessity for framing the kind of propositions that are capable of empirical testing. This means relatively simple problems, carefully defined, with only a few controlled variables, dealing with data that have the qualities of accessibility, permanence, uniformity, and repetitiveness. It is the most highly abstract way of dealing with concrete, i.e., experienceable, reality. It stresses verification by repetition, prediction, application, external and internal logical consistency. It is based on the probability

[200]

calculus; it is actuarial or statistical. It advocates the development of precision instruments for use in observation, recording, and manipulation, as the indispensable prerequisites for sound scientific work in any field. It holds that the history of science is the history of scientific technology. It believes that sound concrete empirical research is both possible and necessary on the level of personal and societal behavior, that these two terms refer to actual isolates, and that research into each will throw light upon the other, as will also research into the biological and physical realms, but that none of these isolates are in any real sense *reducible* to the others, nor logically derivative from them, even though they are organically related. They represent more than a mere arbitrary division of labor, and yet any science will ignore findings in other fields at its peril. The general methods and point of view is the same for all science, though necessarily the particular methods, techniques, and technological devices used will vary greatly with the data being studied. The logic and philosophy of all natural sciences are identical, but any theory of reducibility, identity, and hierarchical ordering is highly suspect. All scientific data are abstractions. Data are not logical; only man is logical—and within only certain limits. It is out of the cumulative findings of such simple, particular, highly abstracted, empirical researches that the material for valid general scientific theories must come. It is by such research only that "causal validity" can be ascertained and upon it, at long last, that all "meaningful validity" must depend.

None of the men in the Conference believe that any of these approaches alone is sufficient for sound research in the social sciences. They all are necessary. Illuminative interpretations, insights, and organizing concepts are the source of hypotheses. Logico-systematic analysis is necessary both before and after empirical research is done. Empirical research is the firm base upon which theories must be erected and is the most definitive and satisfactory means of testing specific hypotheses. Large, general theories cannot be tested or verified by any specific research. They may be "verified," in the sense of becoming generally accepted, as the result of numerous, relevant, specific researches extending over a long period of time until the universe covered by the general theory has been pretty completely exhausted, either actually, or, as is usually the case, inferentially by sampling.

In conclusion, one may say that useful research in the social sciences can be done at any of these four levels; that the results obtained are organically and reciprocally related and must eventually be synthesized with the findings in adjacent fields. However, the trend is clearly toward the type of research called "delimited empirical"; logico-systematic analysis is increasingly dependent upon such research; organizing concepts tend to grow out of such research and to be tested by it in the general manner described. This is a continuous process. The specific researches make imperative the revision of organizing concepts and general theories, and such revision by logico-systematic analysis sets new problems for further empirical research which requires the development of new or improved precision procedures which depend upon the invention of new or improvement of old technological devices of observation, recording, and manipulation, along with new or improved methodological skills and procedures.

Index

Abel, Theodore, mentioned, 130
Abstractions, to simplify complex social data, 119; and empirical research, 200; scientific data are, 201
Abstract theory and precision procedures, 181-182
Acculturation, 139-140
Activity, 20
Actuarial research (see Statistics)
Addams, Jane, mentioned, 103
Allport, Gordon W., remarks of, 114; 121; 125; 144; 145; 158; 160; 163; 164; 171; 172; 173; 178; 180; supplementary statement, 184-186
Amoral attitude of science, 69, 192, 193
Angleworms, I.Q.'s of, 179
Anthropology, verification of theories, 128-129; effect of sociology on, 135
Apperception mass (see "Hunches"; Insight), as research aid, 50, 88, 127
Appetite, as attitude, 20
Appraisal Committee, genesis of, ix-x; selection of research to be appraised, x-xi; criteria of appraisals, xii, 101-102, 193
"Armchair" sociology, revolt against, 192; function of, 199-200
Attitudes (see Values; Subjective aspect), 8; units of social theory, 20-21; blanket term, 21; Blumer's criticism, 24-25; letters and, 37-39; life histories and, 40; temperamental and character, 54-55, 68-69; individualistic, among Poles, 64; Znaniecki's criticism, 92-95; use of, in Polish Peasant, 107-108; measurement of, 124-126; and case histories, 125-126; and frustration, 158; redefinition of, 174; insight and, 194-196
Authority, and research, 146-147; 148;

danger to science, 150-151
Autobiography (see Life histories)

Bain, Read, remarks of, 117; 118; 119; 122; 124; 126; 131; 133; 136; 142; 143; 154; 156; 157; 160; 162; 163; 164; 165; 167; 176; 177; 179; 182; 183; summary and analysis of the Conference, 191-202
Balch, E. G., review cited, 3
Beard, Charles A., mentioned, 162; criticized, 163; his concept of class, 163
Becoming, social, 7; 12; laws of, 13, 63; absence of laws of, 18, 71; Thomas' views on, 83; 189-190
Behavior, and attitudes, 85-86
Benedict, Ruth, mentioned, 138
Biological factor, importance for social research, 186-187
Bluhm, Solomon, review cited, 3
Blumer, Herbert, chosen to appraise The Polish Peasant, xii; his appraisal, 3-81; remarks of, 106-111 (summary of his Appraisal); 112; 113-14; 115; 116; 118; 123; 124; 129; 130; 131; 133; 141; 142; 143; 144; 145; 146; 147; 148; 149; 150; 151; 152; 154; 155; 159; 162; 170
Bohemian personality type, 59
Bujak, F., mentioned, 88
Burgess, E. W., mentioned, 168

Calvinism, and class struggle, 157
Cantril, Hadley, mentioned, 164
Case histories, and attitudes, 125
Causal relations, 13; 18; 120-121
"Causal" validity, 119-120; 201
Causation, 7; 12; 119-120
Chalasinski, Joseph, cited, 89
Chance discoveries, importance of, 179
Change (see also Social Change), 7;

[203]

19-20; 30; 70; and stability, 94; of cultures, 139-140; dynamics of, 165-166

Character attitude, 55

Child, C. M., mentioned, 166

Class, concept of, 157; criteria of, 159; Beard's, 163; Marx's, 163

Class struggle, as organizing concept, 152; validity of the theory, 156-160; ambiguous nature of, 157; as a cult, 160; way of verifying or refuting, 161-162

Coker, Francis W., remarks of, 103; 150

Collective representations, 198

Collective subjective, 122

Common-sense generalizations, 17; 90

Comparative method, 13-14; need for, 72-73; 83; 87

Complexity, of data, 18; of social life related to letters, 35-36; abstraction and manipulation as means of dealing with, 119

Comte, Auguste, mentioned, 197

Concept, defined, 127; advantages and disadvantages of new, 136-137; wide acceptance no test, 153

Conditioning, early, importance of, 187; to symbolic environment, 194

Conduct, and social status, 167

Conference on Blumer's *Analysis*, 101-184; agreements and disagreements of, 183-184, 191-192ff.; hairsplitting, 190; Bain's summary and analysis of, 191-202; all methodological approaches necessary, 201-202

Configurations, perception of, in research, 127

Consciousness, process of, 20-21

Consumer Purchases study, mentioned, 143

Control (see Social Control), as test of validity, 115; 196

Controlled interview, 134-135

Cooley, Charles H., mentioned, 197, 198

Copernican theory, mentioned, 198

Court records, 47

Creative individual, as personality type, 59

Crime, effect of *Polish Peasant* on

problems of, 130

Cults, scientific ideas as, 160, 177, 199; class struggle as, 160

Cultural change, 139-140

Cultural conditioning, and instincts, 155

Culver, Miss Helen, financial aid to Thomas, 103

Curiosity, and research, vii; and new experience, 58; 166-167

Darwin, Charles, mentioned, 165, 177, 178, 179, 198

Darwin, Erasmus, mentioned, 198

Data, physical and social, distinguished, 119; 194

Day, Edmund E., Foreword, vii-xiii

Definition, of situation, 15, 56-57 (see Social Situation); importance of, 122-123; of attitudes, 124-125; defined, 128

Degeneration, 68

Delimited empirical research, 196; 199-202; trend toward, 202

Delinquency, 167

Demand, supply and, misused, 199

Demoralization, 67-69

Derivations, mentioned, 198

Devil, the, mentioned, 199

Disorganization, social, theory of, 62-67; personal, 67-69

Documents (see Human documents)

Durkheim, Émile, mentioned, 198

Ecological studies, and delinquency, 167

Economic determinism, 162-163; bad effect on historical research, 178

Economic man, misused, 199

Economics, laws in, 143

Einstein, Albert, mentiond, 199

Einsteinian theory, mentioned, 198

Embezzlement, prediction of, 168-170; 171

Emotion, as attitude, 21

Empathic identification, 195

Empirical research, 154; 157-158; testing of general theories, 160-161, 164, 177-178; use in history, 176-179; 184; 196; general theory of, 199-202; evil of overemphasis, 199-200; usefulness of, 200-202; trend

toward, 202
Engels, Friederich, mentioned, 159
Engel's laws, mentioned, 143; 148; 149
Environment, symbolic, 194
Evolution, theory of organic, 156; how "proved," 161, 164-166
Experimental method, limitations of, 13-14
Expert, role of, viii

Facts, and hypothesis, 91
Fairchild, H. P., review cited, 3
Familial system-tendency, 12
Family solidarity, 12; of Polish peasants, 64
Faris, Ellsworth, review cited, 3
Fear, instinct of, 15
Feeling, as attitude, 21
Folklore, aridity of, for research on peasant, 104
Folkways and mores, as organizing concept, 152, 198
Fortune, Reo, mentioned, 136
Four wishes (see Wishes)
Fox Indians, cultural transition of, 138-139
Framework of theory, 121-122
Freud, Sigmund, Thomas' "wish" not from, 132; mentioned, 152, 197
Freudian repression, misuse of, 199
Freudianism, mentioned, 156
Fundamental attitudes (wishes), 54-55

Galen, Claudius, mentioned, 180
Gallup, George, mentioned, 126
Galvani, Luigi, mentioned, 166
Gazeta Świąteczna, source materials in, 104
Generalization, viii; 17-18; 75; definition of, 123; in economics and sociology, 141-144; inexact, but useful, 149-150; tested by being broken down, 160; insightful, 197
Genesis, lines of, 40-41; 43; 54
Genius, G. Stein's test for, 141
Germany, and precision instruments, 181; and abstract theories, 182
Giddings, F. H., mentioned, 195
Glueck, Sheldon, mentioned, 168
Goethe, J. W. von, mentioned, 197
Grabski, W., cited, 89

Gresham's law, mentioned, 119-120, 149

Habit, as attitude, 21
Hamilton, G. V., mentioned, 134
Hartman, D. A., mentioned 164
Hate, instinct of, 15
Heraclitean view, mentioned, 94
History, effect of *Polish Peasant* on, 175
History of Medicine, mentioned, 180
Hull House, mentioned, 103
Human documents, use of, 28-53; letters, 29-39; life histories, 39-47; other forms, 47-50; general remarks on, 50-53; interpretation of, 74-78; defects of, 78-81; Thomas' views on, 84-85; and theory, 108-111; as specific instances, 118-119; "perfect" material, 133; spontaneous vs. prepared, 134; not proof of Thomas-Znaniecki's theories, 191
Human nature, stabilities in, 84
"Hunches," 33; 76; sources of, 123; 127; 196-197; give hypotheses, 201
Hypotheses, testing of, 13; facts and, 91; 120; wide acceptance no test, 153; canon of simplicity, 153; alternative, 154; sources of, 87, 201

Ideal-typical analysis, 119-120
Identification, empathic, 195
Illumination, as scientific test, 112-116; 123; and scientific laws, 142-143; 184; general theory of, 196-197; 198; gives hypotheses, 201
Imagination, creative (see Insight; Understanding) 196-198; 200
Immigration, 103; effect of *Polish Peasant* on problems of, 130
Impulse, as attitude, 21; 55
Indirect influences and empirical verification, 163
Individual organization, 8
Individualistic tendencies, 64
Inductive science, and theory, 90-91; procedure of, 91
Inferiority feeling, misused, 199
Insight, 33; 76; 92; 127; 134; 140; 195; general theory of, 196-197; gives hypotheses, 201

Instinct, 15; doctrine of, 112-113; hypothesis of, 155-156; of aggression, 156; misuse of, 199

Institutions, 23

Interaction, between individual and group, 57-58, 60; of attitudes and values, 145; of theory and data, 177; of personal and societal, 201

Interpretation, reasonable, 151-152

Interview, controlled, 134-135

Intuition (see Insight; Understanding; "Hunches")

Irrationalism, in Germany and U. S., 183

Jennings, H. S., mentioned, 166

Jewish Daily Forward, material from, 132

Judgment, as methodological aid, 34, 61, 80-81; 146-147; dangers of, 150-151

Keplerian theory, mentioned, 198

Kornhauser, A. W., mentioned, 158

Kulikowski, Mr., Thomas' assistant, 105

Lamarck, J. B. P. A. M., mentioned, 198

Laws, social, formulation of, 141-142

"Laws of social becoming" (see Becoming, laws of)

Laws of social disorganization (see Disorganization; Reorganization)

Lazarus, Moritz, influence on Thomas, 103

Lerner, Max, remarks of, 111-112; 112-113; 116; 117; 126; 136; 137; 140; 141; 142; 144; 145; 146; 150; 151; 152; 155; 156; 158; 159; 160; 163; 164; 165; 167; 174; 175; 177; 178; 181; 182

Leaders, Polish, 66

Letters, 29-39; "whole" social life, and, 35-36; shortcomings, 36-37; advantages, 37-38

Life histories, 39-46; uses of, 40-42; shortcomings, 43-47, 78; Swedish, 133; and anthropology, 135; and statistics, 171

Life organization, 55-56

Literary insight (see Insight; Illumination)

Loeb, Jacques, mentioned, 166

Logic, in research, 127; 153; 184; may be a fault, 190-191; use of, 199-200; in empirical research, 201

Logico-systematic analysis, 196; general theory of, 199-200

Manipulation, to simplify complex physical data, 119

Marginal utility, law of, mentioned, 148

Marx, Karl, mentioned, 158, 160, 197; concept of class, 163

Mass mind, 185

Mass phenomena generalizations, 17-18

Mastery, wish for, 15

Mead, Margaret, mentioned, 136

Meaning, 25-26; 93; meaning-complex, 120

"Meaningful" validity, 118-119; 147; 201

Mechanics, 16

Methodological formula, 27-28

Methodological Note, writing of, 83; mentioned, 122, 142, 177, 188

Methodological procedure, Thomas' "point to point" view, 166-167; 172; 190-191

Methodological scheme of *Polish Peasant,* 19-20

Methodology, 6-20; central formula, 9; 13-14; letters as device, 32-39; Thomas' idea of, 166-167; differing views of, 183-184; same in "natural" and social sciences, 187-188, 201; "bit-by-bit" view, 190-191

Meyer, Eduard, mentioned, 120

Microscope, importance in medicine, 180

Mores and folkways, as organizing concept, 152; 198

"Motive," as meaning-complex, 120

Murdock, George P., remarks of, 135; 136; 137; 138; 139; 147; 179; supplementary statement, 186-187

Mutuality, 159

Mythical personality, 8

Natural history, of social data, 192
"Natural thing," 22; 55
Negative cases, 13; 18; 161; 200
Negativistic attitude of social sciences, 138
New experience, wish for, 15; 58
Newspaper documents, 47
Newtonian theory, mentioned, 198
Nichols, Roy F., remarks of, 129; 130; 131; 133; 144; 175; 176; 177; 178; 179
"Nonexistent, Book of," 171
Nonmoralistic attitude of social scientist, 193
Nourse, E. G., remarks of, 102-103; 184

Objective, 8; as collective subjective, 122; defined, 196
Objective cultural data (see Values), 8; 70
Ogburn, W. F., mentioned, 180
Organic process, tentative, mentioned, 198
Organizing concepts, and scientific advance, 152-153; 179; 196; general theory of, 197-199; source of, 198; advantages and disadvantages of, 198-199
Only child, misuse of concept, 199

Parental tyranny, 12
Pareto, Vilfredo, mentioned, 198
Parish records, 47
Park, Robert E., mentioned, 166
Participant observers, 133
Pasteur, Louis, mentioned, 180
Pattern, as sociological concept, 95-98; 158; and history, 176
Pawlowski, Josef, interpretation of letter about, 49-50
Perceptual pattern, 127, 128
"Perfect" human document, 39-40; 133
Personal disorganization, 67-69
Personal evolution, 41-42; 54; 57-58
Personal life record (see Life histories)
Personality, development, 41-42; types, 42, 59; theory of, 54-61; types stimulated research, 174
Pfeffer, Wilhelm, mentioned, 166

Philistine personality type, 46; 59
Philology, studied by Thomas, 103
Physical data, distinguished from social, 119; 194
Physics, 16; 94
"Planless" empiricism, 17; 174; 180-181; protection against, 200
Poffenberger, A. T., remarks of, 138
Polish Peasant, The, Conference on, xii-xiii, 101-184; publication note, xv; reviews of, 3; character and purpose, 3-6; influence of, 5-6; methodology, 6-20; social theory of, 20-23, 54-69; criticism of methodology, 24-28; human documents, 28-53; general evaluation, 69-81; conclusions from appraisal, 81-82; contributions, 81-82, 88-90; 129-131; 186-187; 191-193; statement by W. I. Thomas, 82-87; statement by Florian Znaniecki, 87-98; Blumer's summary of his Analysis, 106-111; effect on anthropology and psychiatry, 135; statistical test, 169; as historical interpretation, 173; effect on history, 175; criticism of theory, 188; Bain's summary of Conference on, 191-202
Polish peasant society, sketch of, 30-31; individualistic tendencies, 64; Znaniecki's knowledge of, 106
"Polish Warfare," 104-105
Postulates, importance of, 154; need for explicit, 162; conformity to, as a test, 185; in theoretical analysis, 200
Pragmatic test of validity, 115-116; 184; 197
Precision procedures, in social research, 180; 181; 182-183; 201
Prediction, as criterion of validity, 115-116; of embezzlement, 168-169; 184; actuarial vs. individual, 185; subjective factor and, 195; uniformity of nature, 195; and empirical research, 200-201
Primary data, 8
Primary group, breakdown of Polish, 64-65; as organizing concept, 198
Probability, 84; and causation, 120; 144; and valid generalization, 168-

ganization of, v

Social situation, nature of, 11; definition of, 15, 56-57; criticism, 25-26; meaning of, 195

Social status, and conduct, 167

Social taboos, obstacles to research, 193

Social technician, 11

Social theorist, 11; function of, 199-200; qualifications of, 199-200

Social theory, 7ff.; weaknesses, 10-11; units, 20-21; 23-24; of *Polish Peasant*, 54-69; need for, 72-73; and induction, 90-91; as cults, 160, 177, 199; abstractions and precision tests, 181-182; differing views, 183-184, 194-196; four types, 196-202; verification by theorist, 199-200

Social value (see Values)

Social work, effect of *Polish Peasant* on, 130-131; and insight, 197

Sociographic study, 87

Sociological laws, 144-145

Sociology, and values, 22; effect on history, 175-176; as a natural science, 192

Specific instances, as test of validity of theory, 78-79; 112-114; human documents as, 118-119; and science, 123; not proof of general theory, 161, 202

Spencer, Herbert, influence on Thomas, 103; mentioned, 135, 178, 197

Stability, and change, 94

Stagner, Ross, mentioned, 164

"Standpoint and method," 5-6

Staniewicz, W., mentioned, 89

State Institute for Rural Culture, Warsaw, aided by *The Polish Peasant,* 89

Statistics, as test of human documents, 79; Thomas' views on, 86-87; Blumer's views, 114-115; and "causal" validity, 120; as proof of a theory, 148; and validity of theory, 168-169; and life histories, 171; chief fallacy of, 185; as test of *Polish Peasant* theory, 188-189; and empirical research, 201

Stein, Gertrude, mentioned, 141

Steinthal, Hajim, influence on Thomas, 103

Stouffer, Samuel A., remarks of, 115; 124; 125; 126; 143; 167; 179; 181

Subjective aspect (see Attitudes), 8; 28; and human documents, 51-52; 70; collective subjective, 122; as basis of interpretation, 170; and prediction, 185-186; theory of its unimportance, 187-188; its importance, 194-196

Sumner, William Graham, mentioned 135, 186, 198

"Superior" material, 133

Supply and demand, misuse, 199

Swedish social records, 86; 132-133; as statistical material, 171

Symbols, 194; 196; scientific data as, 201

Symbolic environment, 194

"Symptomatic" events, 120

Synthesis, of empirical findings, 176-179; need for, 183, 201-202

System, as sociological concept, 95-98

Tarde, Gabriel, mentioned, 135, 197

Temperament, 54-55

Temperamental attitudes, 55-56; 68-69

Tendency, as substitute for attitude, 93

Theory (see Social theory)

Thomas, W. I., statement by, 82-87; letter of, quoted, 166-167; remarks of, 102-105; 130; 131; 133; 134; 138; 167; 170; 171; 172; 173; 184

Thompson, Warren S., remarks of, 101; 102; 106; 111; 134; 150; 173; 174; 175; 184

Thrasher, F. M., mentioned, 167

Thurstone, L. L., mentioned, 124-125

Tools, importance of, in research, 180; 201

Traits, 160

Transition, cultural, 30; of Fox Indians, 138-139

Transitional cultures, Polish, 19-20, 30, 70; Fox Indians, 138-139; types of, 197

Turbulences, Giddings', mentioned, 195

Understanding, as result of research, 142; of situation, 195, 197
Uniformity of data, 195
Units of social theory, 20-21
Unpredictability, of social phenomena, 194; of physical and biological, 195
Use of letters (see Letters)

Validity of scientific knowledge, 70; 116-117; verification of general theory of organic evolution, 164-165; general theories and empirical studies, 177-178; 201
Validity of social theory, 75-76; 79; 92; 98; by human documents, 110; 111-129; can there be any?, 117; tests of, 113, 129, 153-154, 184-185; acceptance no test, 137-138, 152-153; objective tests, 147-148; class struggle, 156-160; by statistical analysis, 168-169; role of tools, 180; two views on, 194-196; organizing concepts, 198-199
Validity, tests of, 36, 129; of life histories, 45-46; "causal" and "meaningful," 119-120, 201; of general theories, 161-162, 164
Values (see Attitudes) 8; 19-20; units of social theory, 20-21; criticism, 24-25; and disorganization, 62-63; Znaniecki's criticism, 92-95; 107-108; and wish, 172; relative to atti-

tudes, 194
Variables, controlled, 118; necessity for few, 161, 164, 195, 200-202
Verworn, Max, mentioned, 166
Vold, George B., mentioned, 168
Völkerpsychologie, influence of, on Thomas, 103

Waller, Willard W., remarks of, 115; 126; 129; 130; 131; 140; 152; 153; 162; 179; 183
Weber, Max, quoted, 119-120; relation of Calvinism to capitalism, 157
"Will to power," wish for, 15
Willey, Malcolm M., remarks of, 126; 140; 141; 142; 145; 150; supplementary statement, 187-191
Wirth, Louis, review cited, 3; remarks of, 119; 121; 122; 124; 129; 130; 131; 134; 147; 148; 153; 154; 155; 156; 157; 159; 160; 164; 166; 177; 183
Wirtschaft und Gesellschaft, quoted, 120-121
Wishes (see Attitudes) 15-16; 58ff.; not derived from Freud, 132; and values, 172; a classificatory concept, 173; misuse, 199
Władek, life record of, 42-47; 60-61

Znaniecki, Florian, statement by, 87-98; meets Thomas, 105-106